A to Z 神秘案件

中英双语

第一辑

THE DEADLY DUNGEON
恐怖的地牢

[美] 罗恩·罗伊 著
[美] 约翰·史蒂文·格尼 绘　王芬芬 译

湖南少年儿童出版社　小博集
·长沙·

贝尔法斯特
缅因州

绿地镇

北
西 东
南

侧门

游乐房

通往游乐房的小路

通往缅因州的贝尔法斯特的路

欢迎来到驼鹿庄园
一起解开 A to Z 神秘案件

- 护城河花园
- 城堡
- 大西洋
- 通往海滩的楼梯
- 护城河
- 前门
- 吊桥
- 野餐海滩

人物介绍

三人小组的成员，聪明勇敢，喜欢读推理小说，紧急关头总能保持头脑冷静。喜欢在做事之前好好思考！

丁丁

三人小组的成员，活泼机智，喜欢吃好吃的食物，常常有意想不到的点子。

乔希

三人小组的成员，活泼开朗，喜欢从头到脚穿同一种颜色的衣服，总是那个能找到大部分线索的人。

露丝

沃利斯·华莱士

三人小组的朋友，是一位儿童推理小说作家，邀请他们来自己的城堡做客。

著名儿童推理小说作家沃利斯·华莱士的哥哥，有一艘捕龙虾的船。

沃克·华莱士

里普利·皮尔斯

沃克·华莱士的朋友，也拥有一艘捕龙虾的船，总是把自己的船清扫得很干净。

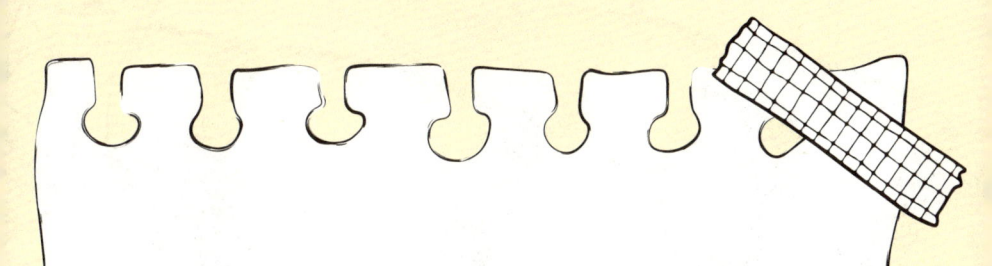

字母 D 代表 dangerous，危险……

丁丁深深吸了一口海边的空气。蓝色的海洋上，点缀着五颜六色的小船。"真美啊！"他说。

乔希小心翼翼地朝悬崖下面看："我们怎么下去啊？"

……………

突然，身后的城堡里传来一声尖叫。

丁丁差点松开了手中握着的野餐篮。他双臂上的皮肤上起了无数鸡皮疙瘩。

沃利斯回头看了一眼，咧嘴笑了："丁丁、乔希和露丝，我给你们介绍……那是埃默里·斯科特的鬼魂！"

第一章

丁丁在座椅上扭来扭去。他和乔希、露丝早上七点就上车了,一直坐到现在。

他们要去缅因州看望朋友沃利斯·华莱士——一名著名的推理小说作家。她来绿地镇时,他们认识了她。丁丁回想起他们从一名"绑匪"手中救下沃利斯的事,不禁笑了起来。

丁丁看了看在座位上睡着的乔希,他的速写本正摊放在腿上。

沃利斯·华莱士

A to Z 神秘案件

露丝坐在乔希后面,正在看地图。她喜欢全身上下穿同一个颜色的衣服。今天她从T恤衫到高帮鞋都是绿色的。

丁丁到露丝身旁坐下。"我们到哪儿了?"他问。

"快到这儿了。"她指着地图上缅因州的贝尔法斯特。"我们刚刚经过'欢迎来到贝尔法斯特'的指示牌。"

丁丁点头。沃利斯会在这里接上他们。

露丝把地图卷起来放进背包。"好兴奋啊!"她说,"你们说,她的城堡里会有护城河和地牢吗?"

"我只希望里面有吃的。"丁丁说,"我快饿死了!"

乔希的脑袋突然出现在他们面前:"我也好饿!到了吗?"

这时,巴士司机大声说:"贝尔法斯特到了!"

"太好了!"乔希边说边跳到巴士过道上。

巴士停在了一栋灰色的小房子前面。透过车

恐怖的地牢

窗，丁丁看见了河水。

"看见沃利斯了吗？"露丝问。

丁丁抓起背包："没看见，先下车吧。我在巴士上待得不舒服！"

孩子们来到车头，跟随一对老夫妇下了车。

他们眯着眼睛，迎着刺眼的阳光，突然听见有人喊："孩子们好啊！"一个有着金色鬈发的高个男子正迎面走来。他的脸被晒得黝黑，但脸上满是笑容。

"我记得您。您是沃利斯的哥哥！"露丝说。

"叫我沃克就行。"男子说，"沃利斯在买食物，所以叫我来接你们。"

沃克·华莱士拎起丁丁的背包，背包重重地撞到沃克的腿上。

"里面是什么，你收集的石头吗？"他问。

丁丁咧嘴一笑："是书。妈妈说缅因州经常下雨，所以我有备而来。"

沃克哈哈大笑："好天气等着你们呢。每天都会阳光灿烂！走吧，我的吉普车在那儿。"

沃克那辆满是灰尘的棕色吉普车是敞篷的，

皮座椅已经泛旧，有些地方都裂开了。

他把后座上的一双鞋和一根工具腰带拨到地上，腾出一些空间。"你们挤一挤！"

男孩们爬到后座，露丝坐在沃克旁边。"城堡有多远？"她问。

"不远。"沃克指着前方说，"穿过树林大约

一英里[1]。"

他沿海岸线开着车,说:"你们饿了吧?我妹妹正在商店给你们买吃的。"

"我总是饿。"乔希说着,往后一仰,跷起二

---

1. 英里:英美制长度单位。1英里=1.6093千米。——编者

A to Z 神秘案件

郎腿。他深深地吸了一口海边的空气:"空气真好啊!"

"喂!"丁丁说,"你的臭脚别放到我面前!"

"我的脚不臭。"乔希说着,举起运动鞋在丁丁鼻子底下晃了晃。

"这是什么?"丁丁从乔希的鞋底拔出一根亮绿色的羽毛。

乔希耸了耸肩:"肯定是我在巴士上踩到的。"

丁丁把羽毛放进自己的口袋。

"那就是驼鹿庄园!"沃克指向树林,大声说道。

丁丁盯着高高的城堡。城堡由灰色的大石头建成。一扇扇小小的黑色窗户看起来像是一双双正盯着人看的眼睛。城堡外围是一圈铁栅栏。

"真酷。"丁丁轻声说。

"快看,护城河!"露丝说。

"那儿有一座吊桥!"乔希激动地说。

沃克把车停在了城堡门口,孩子们拿着背包跳下车。

"我得回我的船上了。"沃克说,"我妹妹应该快回来了。祝你们玩得开心！"他挥挥手，快速穿过树林离开了。

近距离看，城堡高耸在孩子们的头顶，丁丁觉得城堡顶部的城垛就像巨人的牙齿。

乔希推了一下门，门嘎吱嘎吱地打开了。他们低头朝护城河看去。露丝笑出了声："你们看！"

干涸的护城河底部种满了花！

"喂！"乔希大喊，"来看这个！"他已经过了吊桥，站在一扇大木门前面。他用力推门把手，但门纹丝不动。"沃利斯究竟是怎么进到里面的？"

这时，丁丁听见了汽车的响声。一辆红色大众牌敞篷车停在门口。嘟嘟的喇叭声响起，一只手用力地挥舞着。

"是沃利斯！"丁丁大声说。

第二章

"欢迎你们！"沃利斯大声说。

她还是丁丁印象中的样子：快乐的笑容、棕色的鬈发和淘气的眼神。

"你们觉得驼鹿庄园怎么样？"她问，"好玩吗？"

"我喜欢这里！"露丝说。

"这里超级棒！"乔希说。

沃利斯笑了："还不错，对吧？帮我拿一下这些吃的，我带你们好好参观一番！"

恐怖的地牢

原来拐角处有一扇普通大小的门,那就是城堡的入口。沃利斯和孩子们拎着大包小包的东西,来到一个大房间。丁丁看见一台洗衣机和一台烘干机,挂衣帽的木质挂钩,以及一堆运动鞋和靴子。

"这儿是换鞋室。"沃利斯说,"从这儿过去是厨房。"她用屁股顶开另一扇门。

天花板非常高,丁丁得仰着头看。厨房的物品一应俱全,屋子中间摆了一张长长的木头桌子。桌子上方悬挂着一个黑色枝形吊灯。

"这里真大啊!"丁丁说。

"所以我喜欢这里。"沃利斯说,"把食物放下,我带你们四处走走。"

沃利斯把牛奶和冰激凌放进冰箱,孩子们则快速把袋子里的食物拿出来。

"好了,从气派的客厅开始参观。"沃利斯说,"跟我走!"她带着孩子们走进客厅,丁丁第一次见到这么大的客厅。

丁丁最先注意到的是头顶悬挂的枝形吊灯,它有沃利斯的汽车那么大!

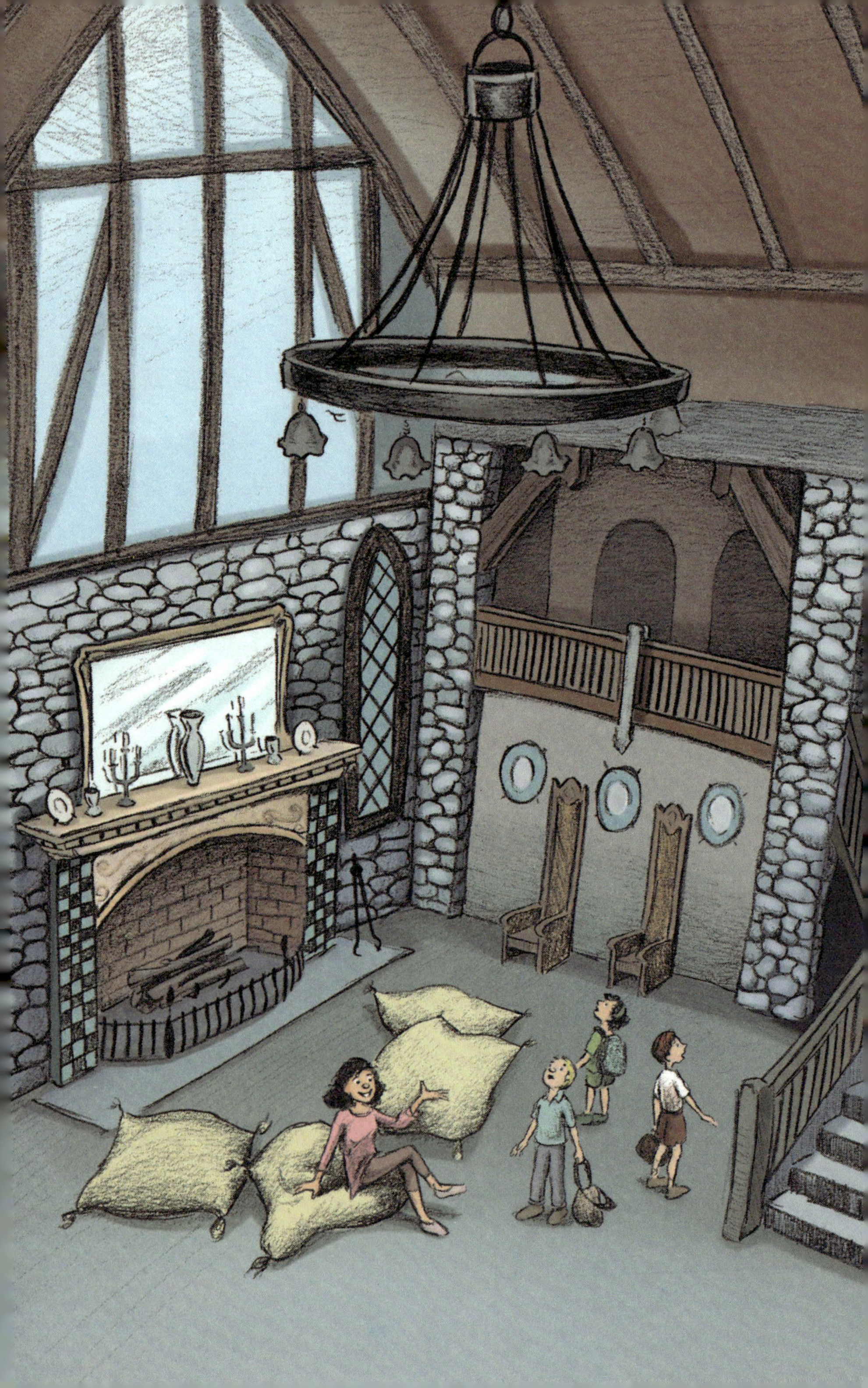

恐怖的地牢

大理石壁炉几乎有整面墙壁那么大。壁炉架由深色木头制成,上面雕刻了各种动物的图案。

"这个地方太震撼了!"丁丁说。

"天哪!"乔希向壁炉里看去,轻声说,"这里面可以烧整整一棵树!"

沃利斯坐在一堆地垫上。"冬天的某些时候,我倒是真想烧一整棵树。"她说,"这悬崖上越来越冷了。"

"这座城堡建成多少年了?"露丝一边问,一边抬头看向高高的石头墙壁。

"很多年了。"沃利斯说,"二十世纪三十年代,影星埃默里·斯科特建造了这里。"

"真令人惊讶!"乔希说。

"他怎么了?"丁丁问。

"嗯……"沃利斯扬起眉毛,压低了声音,"镇上的人说他突然死了,就死在这座城堡里。说实话,我有时都觉得能听见他的鬼魂在哀鸣!"

孩子们吓得目瞪口呆。

随即丁丁笑了:"哎呀,您是开玩笑的,对吧?"

"怎么了?你们不信有鬼魂吗?"沃利斯笑

19

着问。

"不信!"孩子们异口同声。

"好吧……"沃利斯站起来,"也许埃默里做好准备后,会向你们做自我介绍。来吧,跟我去看你们的房间。"

孩子们抓起背包,跟随沃利斯走上通往二楼的宽大石板楼梯。楼梯尽头是一条昏暗的走廊,走廊上有几扇房门。

沃利斯指着其中一扇门:"这是我的房间。露丝,那是你的房间;两个男孩,睡走廊对面的房间。"

沃利斯轻轻拍了一下走廊尽头的一扇窄门:"这扇门通往屋顶。"

丁丁打开他们的卧室门。和楼下的房间一样,卧室的天花板也很高。石板地面上铺着一张蓝色地毯。两张单人床上铺着亮红色床罩。

丁丁走到窗户边朝外看,只看见一片片的松树。"大海在哪儿?"他问。

"在另一边。"沃利斯说,"你们先休息一下,一会儿下来吃午餐。"

露丝进了她的卧室。丁丁和乔希把背包扔在床上。

"这里真不错。"乔希边说边走进浴室。

丁丁把自己带的书堆放到床边的桌子上。他一把脱掉衣服,换上短裤和T恤衫。

"丁丁,快过来!"乔希叫道。

丁丁走进浴室。

"听!"乔希说。他的一只耳朵贴在浴室的一面墙壁上。

"你在干什么?"丁丁问。

乔希嘘了一声:"我好像听见了什么声音!"

"怎么了?"露丝走进房间,问道。

"乔希说他听见墙后面有声音。"丁丁答。

露丝咧嘴笑了:"一定是埃默里·斯科特的鬼魂在叫。他正等着你们俩今晚入睡呢!"

这时他们听到沃利斯的声音。"下楼来拿东西!"她喊道。孩子们跑下楼去厨房。

沃利斯正在往篮子里装东西。"天气这么好,我们应该去海滩野餐。"她说。

"太好了!"乔希说,"我们可以找个时间去钓鱼吗?"

沃利斯点点头:"问问沃克能否借一些渔具给你们。其实,他明天会带你们去捕龙虾。"

"好棒!"乔希欢呼。

沃利斯笑了:"明早四点半出发,你就不会这么想了。"

丁丁和乔希各抓着篮子的一端。沃利斯递给露丝一块野餐垫,带着他们来到城堡后面,穿过另外一扇门走了出去。

"景色优美,对吧?"沃利斯说,"我第一次看见这个地方,就想在这儿进行写作。"

丁丁深深吸了一口海边的空气。蓝色的海洋上,点缀着五颜六色的小船。"真美啊!"他说。

乔希小心翼翼地朝悬崖下面看:"我们怎么下去啊?"

沃利斯笑着说:"看见那边了吗?我修了台阶。你们记得城堡里宽大的壁炉和庞大的吊灯吗?每一件都是用小船从欧洲运过来的。唉,埃默里·斯科特真是不容易!天知道他是怎么把东西搬上这悬崖峭壁的!"

突然,身后的城堡里传来一声尖叫。

丁丁差点松开了手中握着的野餐篮。他双臂的皮肤上起了无数鸡皮疙瘩。

沃利斯回头看了一眼,咧嘴笑了:"丁丁、乔希和露丝,我给你们介绍……那是埃默里·斯科特的鬼魂!"

第三章

孩子们默默地盯着沃利斯。

她朝他们眨了眨眼睛:"别怕,这是他打招呼的方式。我们下去吧?"

孩子们面面相觑,跟着沃利斯走下木头台阶。下面是一片小小的沙滩。

丁丁和乔希把篮子放在几块岩石的阴影处,沃利斯和露丝则摊开野餐垫。

"看!那儿有一个洞穴!"乔希说着,指向悬崖底部的一条地道。海水蜿蜒着流进黑乎乎的洞里,形成一条窄窄的小河。

"这个洞穴有多深?"乔希一边问,一边朝漆黑的洞里看。

"我不知道。"沃利斯答道,"沃克告诉我里面有很多蝙蝠。"

他们的野餐食物有鸡肉三明治、苹果、巧克

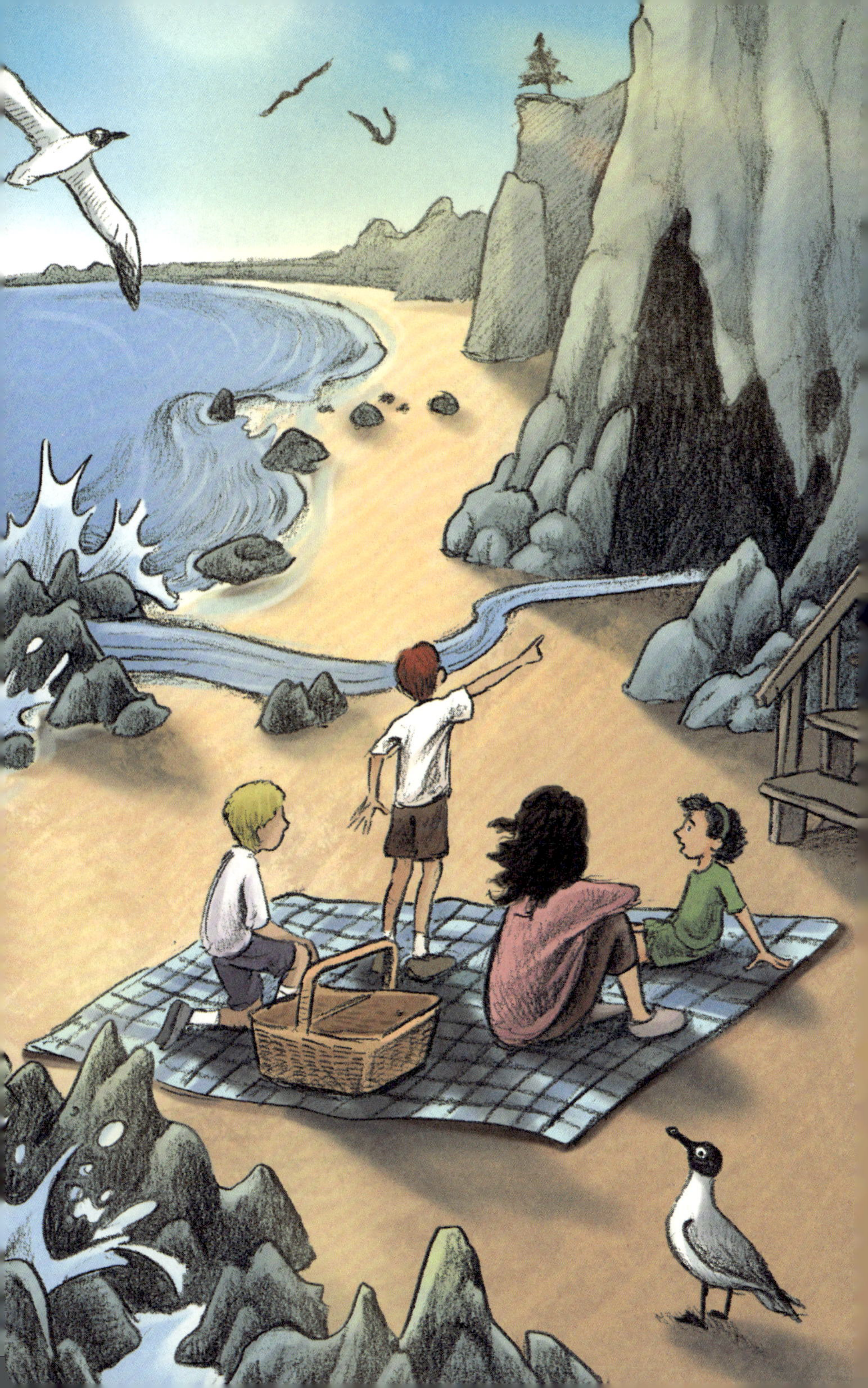

力饼干和冰柠檬水。沃利斯指着海岸线："沃克家就在那片树林里。"

"他去哪儿了？"丁丁问。

"开船出海了。"沃利斯说着，拿起一块饼干指着大海，"大约半英里范围内的深水区都有他捕龙虾的笼子。"

"他怎么找到那些笼子呢？"乔希问。

沃利斯用纸巾擦了擦手："他的小船'幸运女神'号配有高端指南针，而且他很熟悉这片海域。"

野餐结束后，沃利斯把东西全都装回篮子里。"我们去走一走吧？"

他们沿着礁石嶙峋的沙滩走着。露丝走进潮池，在里面捡贝壳。乔希把自己的鞋子挂在脖子上，沿着海岸线蹚水。

"注意龙虾。"丁丁打趣道，"它们可喜欢臭脚丫了。"

乔希咧嘴笑了，把水花泼洒到丁丁身上。

沿着海岸线绕了一个弯后，沃利斯指向前方说："那儿就是沃克家。"

恐怖的地牢

那是一栋有着红色屋顶的灰色小别墅,周围有很多沙丘草和沙子。

这时,他们听见有人在叫喊。丁丁环顾四周,看见有人正在码头尽头挥手。

沃利斯挥手回应:"孩子们,走,认识一下我们的朋友里普利·皮尔斯。"

他们走上码头,走向码头尽头处拴着的一条长长的绿色小船。小船上的黄铜和木制装饰,在阳光的照射下闪闪发亮。

小船旁边站着一名男子,他的手里拿着一块正在滴水的海绵。男子有一双蓝色眼睛和一头顺滑的黑发。

"你好,里普[1]。"沃利斯说,"这是丁丁·邓肯,乔希·平托和露丝·罗斯·哈撒韦。"

男子满脸笑容,伸出一只手。他洁白的牙齿亮闪闪的,肌肤被晒成了古铜色。"你们是这位女士的书迷吧?"

"她的书我全买了!"丁丁大声说。

---

1. 里普(Rip),里普利(Ripley)的昵称——编者

"我在康涅狄格州认识了他们。"沃利斯解释道,"他们来城堡待一周。今晚过来一起吃晚餐吧!"

"我喜欢您的小船。"露丝说,"洁净闪亮!"

里普咧嘴一笑:"谢谢夸赞,小淑女。晚上吃饭见。"

随即他看向乔希。"愿意帮我解开绳子吗?"他指着码头尽头拴着的一根绳子问道。

乔希解开绳子,递给里普。

"很高兴认识你们。"里普说完,上了船,启动马达。小船平稳地驶离了码头。

丁丁望着破水前进的小船,说:"或许,我长大后不会成为一名作家。我想拥有一艘捕龙虾的船。"

沃利斯笑着对丁丁说:"最好坚持写作,丁丁。缅因州的龙虾越来越少了。"

"我迫不及待想登上沃克的小船了。"露丝说。

"我哥哥的船跟里普的可不一样。"沃利斯边说边摇头,"不知道里普怎么把船保持得这么干净。沃克的船一看就是捕龙虾的,一股龙虾味。"

他们转身朝野餐的地方走去。乔希把水踢到露丝身上,露丝大呼小叫,追着他在沙滩上跑。

丁丁和沃利斯一路上安静地走着。他们头顶上有一只海鸥在叫。

丁丁抬头看着沃利斯:"您真的认为我们听见的那声尖叫是埃默里·斯科特的鬼魂在叫吗?"

沃利斯哈哈大笑:"反正自打我住在这里就一直能听见那些叫声。第一次听见时,我把城堡搜了个遍,什么也没发现。"

丁丁打了个寒战。"您经常听见那样的声音吗?"他问。

沃利斯耸了耸肩:"有时几周都没有一点声音,有时连续几天都能听见。"

沃利斯低头笑着对丁丁说:"说实话,丁丁,这个谜团难倒我了。如果那些叫声不是埃默里·斯科特的鬼魂发出的,那会是什么发出的呢?"

第四章

悬崖顶上，沃利斯拿着野餐用的东西。"我要去写我的新书。"她说，"你们为什么不四处逛逛呢？树林里有一间游乐房，是埃默里·斯科特给他的孩子们建的。你们可能会想去看看。"

她打开侧门。"噢，我差点忘了！"她眨巴着眼睛说，"有些人认为他的鬼魂在游乐房附近徘徊，寻找他的孩子们。你们要睁大眼睛哟！"说完，她就进屋里去了。

孩子们在树林中找到了一条小路。丁丁一边

恐怖的地牢

走,一边把沃利斯在海滩上说的话告诉了乔希和露丝。

"真的有鬼?!"乔希说,"好吓人!"

"胡说!"露丝说,"我不相信有鬼。可能是一只动物被困在城堡的某个地方了。"

"不知道。"丁丁说,"沃利斯说她找遍了整座城堡,什么都没发现。"

"况且,"乔希说,"什么动物会发出那样可怕的叫声呢?"

这时,孩子们到了游乐房。小木屋的外墙被刷成和沃利斯的城堡一样的颜色。一座供孩子通过的吊桥,跨越一条浅浅的护城河,通往大门。

"太棒了!"乔希说。

"我们进去吧!"露丝兴奋地大声说着,朝大门跑去。她用力转动门把手,门咔的一声开了。

露丝行屈膝礼:"请进,忠诚的骑士们!"

"让国王陛下丁丁先进。"丁丁说着,挤到乔希前面。

他们挤进了房间。所有东西上都布满灰尘。一点微弱的光从结满蜘蛛网的两扇小窗户透了

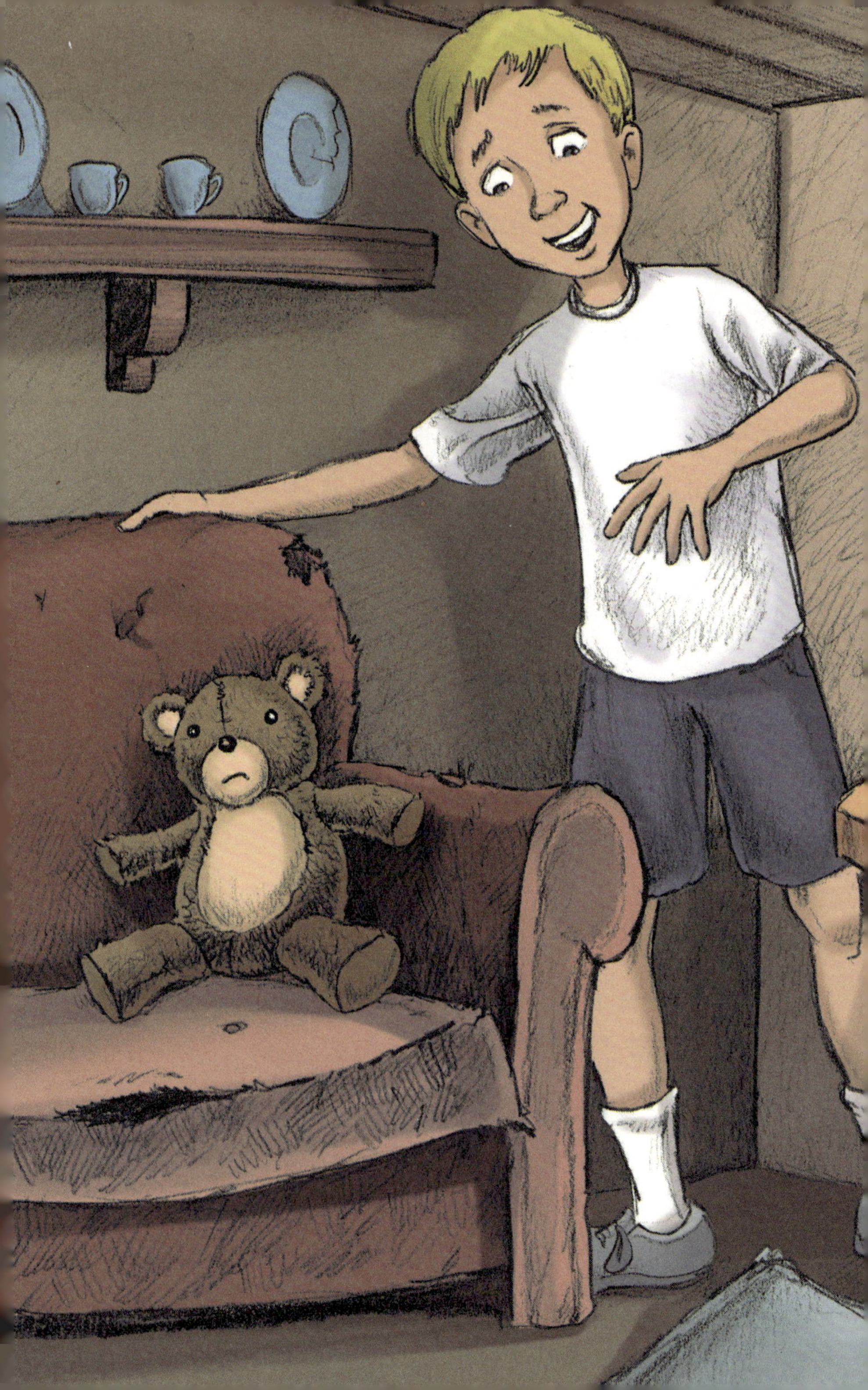

进来。

乔希搓着胳膊。"天哪,这里好冷啊!"他说。

"看起来很多年没人来过这儿了。"露丝说。

屋子中间的地上放了一块脏兮兮的旧地毯,上面摆了一张圆桌和两把小椅子。架子上面有一套小号的蓝色餐具。架子下面,一个孤独的泰迪熊玩偶坐在旧沙发上。

"我觉得这里好吓人。"乔希说。

"快看!"丁丁说,"地毯上有很多脚印。"他踩在一个脚印上,"留下脚印的人肯定有一双大脚!"

"鬼魂会留下脚印吗?"乔希问。

"可能是沃克的。"露丝说,"沃利斯的脚没这么大。"

"但沃克来这儿干吗?"丁丁大声问出自己的疑虑。

"我们走吧?"乔希请求道,"我刚才看见了一只大蜘蛛,它正盯着我看呢!"

"走吧,我们以后再来。"露丝说,"到时候我想把这儿打扫干净。这儿到处都是灰尘,看着不舒服。"

露丝关上门。过吊桥时,丁丁看见护城河里有个东西。于是他跳下去,捡起一根亮绿色的羽毛。

"你们看!像是粘在乔希鞋上的那种羽毛。"

露丝举起羽毛,迎着太阳光仔细观察:"这是什么羽毛?"

恐怖的地牢

乔希仔细瞧了瞧。"我只知道鹦鹉有这样的羽毛。"他说,"但是缅因州没有鹦鹉。"

丁丁从乔希手里拿回羽毛,放进了自己的口袋。

"好了,游乐房看完了。"乔希说,"现在该做我想做的事了。"

丁丁乐呵呵地看着他:"你想吃东西?"

"不是。我想去海滩上的那个洞穴看看。"

"等一下。"丁丁说,"你在游乐房都觉得害怕,竟然想去洞穴看看?"

"洞穴很好玩的。"乔希说,"快走吧。"

孩子们经过城堡,穿过大门,走下悬崖。他们站在洞口,看着从洞穴中流出的小河。"不知道里面的水有多深。"丁丁说。

"这好办。"乔希说。他走进水里,蹚水进了洞穴。水刚刚没过他的脚踝。

"快来啊!"他回头呼喊。

丁丁和露丝跟在他后面。洞穴里越来越暗,直到日光彻底消失。空气阴冷潮湿,黑色的洞壁摸起来黏糊糊的。

"乔希，这水太冰了。"露丝的声音听起来沉闷空洞，"我不想待在这儿了！我们可以回去吗？"

"水也越来越深了。"丁丁说，"我都跟不上你们了！"

"嘘！"乔希示意，"我听见了什么声音！"

"乔希，你别吓我们啊！"露丝说，"我都快——"

突然一声尖叫在洞穴里回荡。

"快跑！"露丝大叫。

在他们的头顶上，成百只黑蝙蝠朝着外面的日光疾飞。

第五章

孩子们一直跑，跑到悬崖顶才停下。丁丁瘫倒在地上，大口喘着粗气。

"刚才是什么声音？"露丝问着，脱下湿透的鞋子，"吓得我心跳都要停止了！"

"是鬼！"乔希说，"我敢说那个洞穴通往城堡下面的秘密地牢。埃默里·斯科特也许就是在那儿丧命的！"

露丝哈哈大笑起来。乔希不理会她继续说："肯定有一扇暗门通往地牢。我要找到这扇门！"

"或许你能找到。"丁丁说,"但我要去洗澡换衣服。"

"我也是。"露丝说,"一身的鱼腥味!"

他们回到城堡时,沃克的吉普车停在大门前。孩子们换上干净的衣服后,下楼来到厨房。沃利斯、沃克和里普正坐在长桌子旁剥玉米。

"嘿,孩子们,"沃克说,"在驼鹿庄园的第一天过得怎么样?"

"开心极了!"乔希说着,给丁丁使了个眼色,"我们去了游乐房,在海滩上发现了一些奇妙的东西。"

丁丁明白,乔希不想让他说出"秘密地牢"

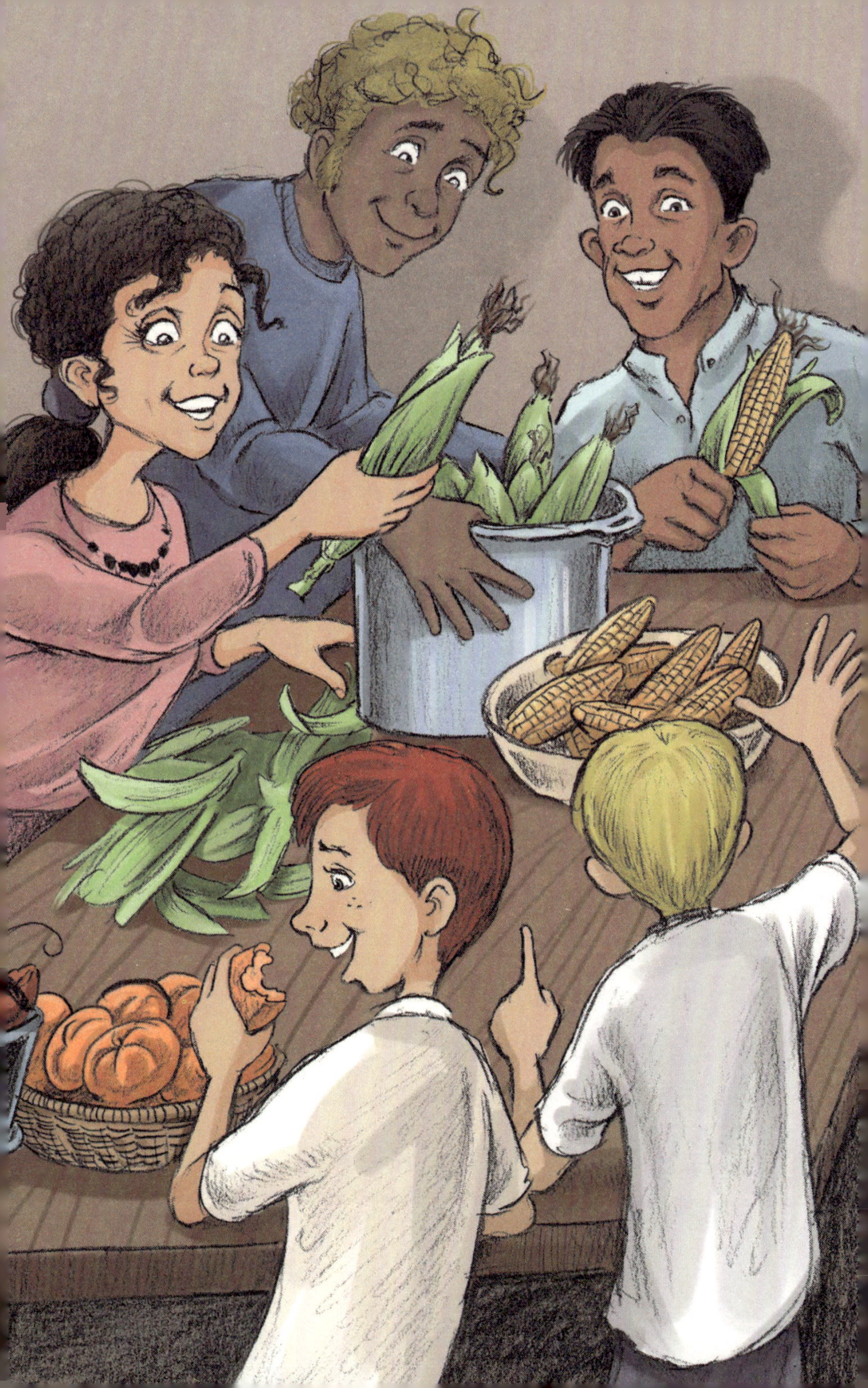

的事。

"好了，我要去烧龙虾。"沃利斯说，"希望你们都饿了！"

吃过晚餐，大人们决定玩拼字游戏。

"孩子们和我们一起玩吧，"沃利斯说，"或者从客厅柜子里拿其他的桌游玩。随你们自己。"

"嗯……我想上楼去看书。"乔希说。他示意丁丁和露丝跟他上楼。随即三人在楼上卧室之间的走廊上会面了。"趁他们在玩拼字游戏，我们搜索一遍这个地方吧。"乔希说。

"到底要找什么？"丁丁问。

"找暗门或秘密通道。"乔希说着，用指关节轻轻敲击着墙壁。

"乔希，沃利斯怎么不告诉我们有暗门呢？"露丝问。

"她可能不知道。"乔希答。

"我认为我们应该四处瞧瞧，"丁丁赞同道，"找出是什么东西发出的那些诡异的声响。"

"从屋顶开始找吧。"露丝说。

他们顺着走廊走，乔希推开了那扇窄门。

恐怖的地牢

走到楼梯顶端,他们打开了另一扇门。来到平坦的楼顶,一阵凉爽的微风迎面吹来。

"哇!视野开阔!"乔希赞叹,"在这儿放风筝真不错!"

丁丁站在两堵比他还高的花岗岩城垛之间,感觉自己像国王在俯瞰自己的国土。

"这里什么也没有。"乔希说。

"是的。"丁丁说,"去楼下看看。"

孩子们又咚咚咚下楼,回到走廊。

露丝进了自己的房间,丁丁和乔希搜索他们的房间。丁丁先查看了柜子,只看见一层灰尘和一把旧网球拍。

他拿起拍子戳了戳窗帘后面。几只蜘蛛爬走了,其他什么也没有。

突然,乔希在浴室里大叫:"丁丁,我被抓住了!救救我!"

丁丁手持网球拍冲进浴室。他四处张望,但里面什么都没有。

"乔希?你在哪儿?"

浴帘被拉开。乔希站在那儿,笑着说:"嘘!"

丁丁摇了摇头："真幼稚，乔希。你就该被鬼抓住！"

乔希从浴缸里爬出来："我以为你不信有鬼呢，丁丁！"

丁丁只是再次摇头。他走到走廊对面，敲了敲露丝的门。"找到什么了吗？"他问。

她摇头："没有。"

她和丁丁搜查了长长的走廊，他们查看了所有暖气片的背面、花盆的里面，还有一个高高的雨伞架。

乔希轻轻敲击着墙壁，想听听有没有空洞的响声。最后他们满头大汗、一身灰尘，只好放弃。

"不知道还要去哪儿找。"丁丁说。

"我们没有找楼下的房间。"乔希说。

"等明天再找吧。"露丝打着哈欠说，"我要去睡觉了。都是因为乔希·平托，但愿我不会梦见鬼。"

乔希笑着说："我看书上说，鬼会吃鬈发的女孩。"

"那就让鬼来试试！"她说完，随即关上了她

恐怖的地牢

的房门。

丁丁和乔希爬上床,不一会儿就睡着了。

突然,丁丁醒了,心脏怦怦直跳。他看了一眼闹钟。此时是午夜!

丁丁下了床,踮起脚走到窗户边,只看见黑漆漆的天空下,一片黑压压的树。

然后他看见——在游乐房附近,有一点诡异的亮光。

第六章

丁丁倒吸一口气,感觉双腿上都起了鸡皮疙瘩。那是不是埃默里·斯科特的鬼魂?

亮光闪了几下,随即消失了。

丁丁打了个寒战,揉了揉眼睛。亮光没有再出现,他又上了床。

他打了个哈欠,闭上了眼睛,以为自己只是看见了一只萤火虫。

正要睡着时,丁丁又睁开了眼睛。他刚才只看见黑暗中有一点亮光在移动。

树林里怎么会只有一只萤火虫呢?他一直在想这个问题,想着想着就睡着了。

丁丁梦见自己又进了那个洞穴,里面一片漆黑,他的头顶传来可怕的尖叫声。但这次,尖叫声没有停止,反而越来越响。突然,他面前飞来了好多蝙蝠。这些蝙蝠都长着羽毛——亮绿色的羽毛!

丁丁腾的一下坐起来。他的双腿被毯子裹着,闹钟正响个不停。

"我不是在洞穴里。"丁丁意识到,"我还在城堡里。"他放心了,关掉闹钟。

"乔希,起床!"他叫着。

乔希睁开了一只眼睛:"为什么?"

丁丁下了床:"沃克要带我们去捕龙虾,还记得吗?"他打开灯,猛地掀开乔希的被子。

"快点,去捕龙虾了!"

乔希小声地抱怨着,但还是起来了:"我讨厌龙虾。"

丁丁笑了。"你昨晚还吃了一只呢。"他穿上昨天的牛仔裤,在T恤衫外面套了一件长袖运动衫,"我现在下楼。别再睡了啊!"

丁丁来到走廊对面,轻轻敲响露丝的房门。她已经起床了,身上穿的戴的都是黄色的。

"你昨晚看见奇怪的东西了吗?"丁丁问。

露丝正在梳头。她摇了摇头当作回答。

"好吧,我看见了!到了楼下告诉你。"

厨房亮着灯。丁丁看见桌上摆了几杯果汁、几碗燕麦片和一些松饼。他正狼吞虎咽时,露丝和乔希来了。

"伙伴们,我觉得昨晚有人在外面鬼鬼祟祟的。"丁丁说道。他把树林里那点亮光的事告诉了大家。

乔希抓起一块松饼,咬掉了一半。

"我早就说过,"他一边吃一边说,"那是埃默里的鬼魂!"

"你真逗,乔希。"露丝说。

突然,从换鞋室传来砰的一声响,厨房门被撞开了。乔希差点从椅子上掉下去。

沃克进来了,穿着一件黄色雨衣和一双高筒橡胶靴。"准备好出发了吗?"他问。

丁丁松了一口气，笑呵呵地说："乔希还以为是鬼来了呢。"

"才不是呢。"乔希咕哝着。

他们走到门口，爬进沃克的吉普车。天空漆黑一片。丁丁盯着树林里看，想要再次看见那点亮光。

几分钟后，沃克拐进了自家的车道。一行人下了车，从房子后面走到码头。他们的鞋子踩在码头的木板上，嘎吱作响。

"看着点路，小心点。"沃克提醒着，还用手电筒照着丁丁脚下。

夜晚的空气中夹杂着咸味，丁丁大口呼吸着。小船上方泛起点点星光。他听见一只夜莺在某处鸣叫。

"你们准备好上船了吗？"沃克问。

丁丁、乔希和露丝，跟随沃克登上了笼罩在夜色中的船。

第七章

"最好穿上救生衣。"孩子们上船后,沃克指着挂在一排挂钩上的橙色救生衣说道。

孩子们穿上肥大的救生马甲,坐在长凳上。沃克启动马达,小船驶离了码头。

"大约一个小时后到达我的捕虾笼。"沃克在马达的轰鸣声中大声说,"你们休息一下。"

露丝和乔希蜷缩在长凳上,丁丁却坐得直直的。他不想错过任何事情。他闻到了龙虾饵料的味道。他们在漆黑的水面颠簸前行时,波浪拍

恐怖的地牢

打着船身。

丁丁看见晨晖将天际染成了淡黄色，这让他想起来昨晚看见的光。那点亮光与怪异的声音或两根亮绿色的羽毛有关系吗？

小船轻轻摇晃，丁丁昏昏欲睡。他闭上了双眼，后来沃克把他摇醒。丁丁坐直身子，眯着眼睛看向太阳。

小船在波浪中摇摇晃晃，丁丁起身时差点没站稳。"我们到哪儿了？"他问。

"走了大约五英里。"沃克说，"你叫醒露丝和乔希，我们吃点东西。"

他们坐在一缕阳光中。早餐是花生酱三明治和沃克保温瓶里的热牛奶可可。

丁丁看见远处还有一些小船，问道："那些都是捕龙虾的船吗？"

沃克点点头："大部分都是，也有少量捕鱼船。"

乔希从侧面看过去。"您是怎么捕龙虾的？"他问。

沃克指着一台机器说："那台绞车会把龙虾弄上来。一会儿我演示给你们看。"

49

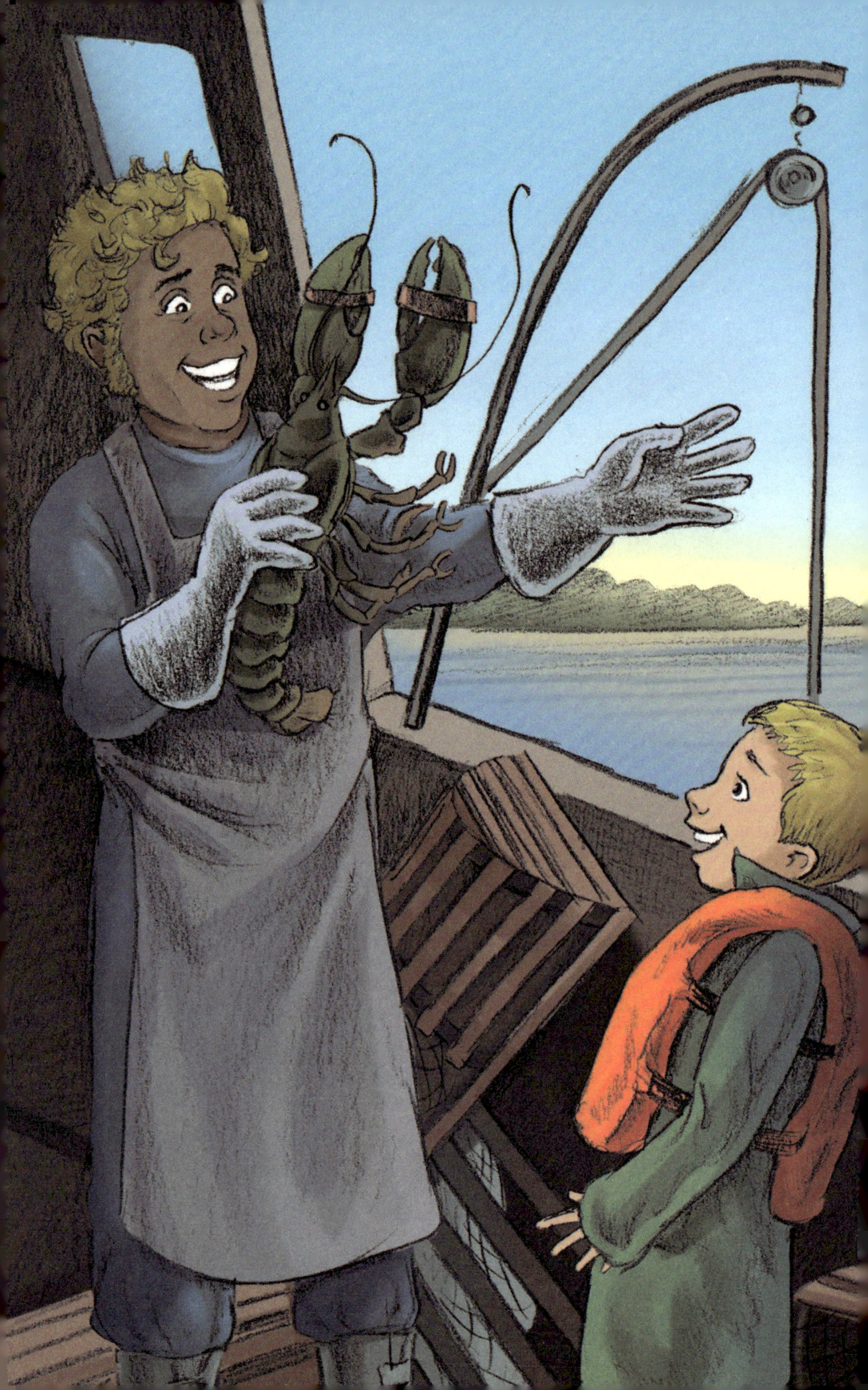

沃克拿起一端有弯钩的长杆，勾住系在浮标上的绳子，把绳子挂在绞车上，按下按键，湿绳子嗖的一声从水里被拉出来。速度好快！

　　几秒钟后，绳子另一端的捕虾笼浮出水面。沃克穿好橡胶围裙，戴好橡胶手套，把捕虾笼拖到小船上。

木笼子上面全是水草。一些小螃蟹爬到甲板上。"看看我们捕到什么了。"沃克说着,把螃蟹扔回海里。

沃克打开笼子的小门,把一只戴着手套的手伸进去,抓出一只湿淋淋的深绿色龙虾。龙虾生气地挥舞着钳子。

"这对钳子能夹断手指。"沃克提醒道。他用两条厚实的橡皮筋绑住龙虾的钳子,随后把龙虾放进一个盛有海水的箱子里。

"乔希,去拿诱饵,好吗?"

乔希把那个重重的桶拖了过来。沃克拿出一个大鱼头。

"哎呀!"乔希说,"真恶心!"

"龙虾可不介意。"沃克说着,把鱼头放进捕虾笼,关紧小门,然后随手又把笼子放回海里。

"龙虾就是这么捕的。"沃克说着,拍掉手套上的水。

"我们可以再拉一个捕虾笼上来吗?"丁丁问道。

"当然可以,你们能帮上忙。到那个柜子里

恐怖的地牢

拿几双手套。"

露丝拿了三双厚实的橡胶手套。沃克用绞车拉出另一个笼子，拿出一只扭来扭去的龙虾递给乔希。

"捏住它的背部，就不会被钳子钳到。"

乔希戴着手套，双手捏住龙虾。露丝和丁丁用橡皮筋绑住龙虾的钳子。

"谁想往这个笼子里放饵料？"沃克笑着问。

乔希假装发出呕吐的声音，丁丁则自告奋勇。他把一只手伸进饵料桶，拿出一个血淋淋的鱼头放进捕虾笼。

早晨渐渐暖和了，孩子们脱下长袖运动衫。大海风平浪静。海鸥在他们头顶盘旋，寻找残羹剩饭。

"看，里普来了。"沃克说。

里普把船停在"幸运女神"号旁边。两艘船并排时，里普扔给丁丁一根缆绳。

"怎么样啊？"里普问。他穿着干净的牛仔裤和T恤衫，一只手端着咖啡杯。

"捕到了一些。"沃克回答，"这几个船员帮了大忙。"

"您准备捕龙虾吗？"乔希问。

里普摇了摇头，露出一抹笑容："今天不捕，孩子们。我只是出来检查一下浮标。把缆绳扔给我，好吗？"

丁丁把缆绳的一端朝旁边的船扔过去。里普用空着的那只手接住了。"祝你们玩得开心！"他大声说着，开船走了。

"谁还要可可？"沃克问。

"我要。"乔希说。

丁丁转过身，看见"幸运女神"号的甲板上有什么东西。

那是一根亮绿色羽毛。

第八章

丁丁捡起了羽毛。露丝扬起眉毛,表示不解。丁丁耸了耸肩,把羽毛放进口袋里。

"准备好出发了吗?"沃克问,"我答应了我妹妹,午餐前带你们回去。"

他启动马达,船嗒嗒嗒地朝陆地驶去。

回到沃克的码头,孩子们帮忙把鱼身上的黏液和海草从小船的甲板上冲掉。随后沃克开车送他们回城堡。

"我妹妹开车出去了。"沃克说,"她一定出去办事了。你们在这儿等一会儿,没问题吧?"

"我有点饿了。"乔希笑着说。

"给你,把这些吃完。"沃克递给乔希面包、花生酱和小刀。他向他们挥手告别,然后开车走了。

"我在哪儿吃呢?"乔希问。

"去游乐房吧?"露丝说,"正好我去清洗一下那些小餐具。"她在换鞋室旁边找到一个喷水壶,在水龙头处接满了水。

在去游乐房的路上,丁丁从口袋里拿出那几根羽毛。他告诉乔希,第三根是在沃克的小船上捡到的。

孩子们仔细研究羽毛,将它们举起来对着太阳看。"这三根羽毛完全一样。"乔希说。

"又是一根鹦鹉羽毛吗?"露丝问,"从哪儿来的呢?"

乔希笑着说:"从鹦鹉身上来的呗!"

"你太逗了,乔希。"

丁丁突然想起自己做过的梦——长着绿色羽毛的蝙蝠在尖叫……

恐怖的地牢

露丝打开游乐房的门,三人进入屋内。

"这儿太冷了。"乔希说,"为什么不在外面的太阳底下吃呢?"

丁丁帮乔希把桌子抬到外面。

露丝把餐具拿到外面,摆在草地上。

"地毯上看起来有好多灰尘,"丁丁说,"我们应该把它拖到外面清洗干净。"

桌边的乔希正忙着把花生酱抹到面包上面:"我们吃完再清洗吧?我的肚子咕咕叫了。"

丁丁跪在地上,开始卷地毯,说:"你的肚子——嘿,快来看!"

"但愿不是另一根绿色羽毛。"乔希喃喃地说着,慢慢走过去看。

丁丁指着地板上的一扇活板门。

"噢!"乔希大声说,"我告诉过你们!有一扇暗门通往秘密地牢!"

露丝跑了过去。"我们把门打开!"她说。

门把手上有一个弹簧锁。露丝按下弹簧,锁砰的一声打开了。三人一起用力拉,活板门打开了。只听呼的一声,湿冷的空气一下子冲了出来，令人毛骨悚然。

"呸，好难闻的气味！"乔希说。

孩子们盯着这个传出难闻气味的洞。石阶一路向黑暗处延伸。虽然光线昏暗，他们还是看见了石阶上的脚印。

"像地毯上的脚印。"丁丁说。

这时，空洞的尖叫声从黑洞里传了出来，他们全都被吓得往后跳。

第九章

"下面有什么东西!"露丝小声说。

乔希瞪大了双眼。"不是什么'东西',"他低声说,"是人,是埃默里·斯科特的鬼魂!"

丁丁把一只手伸进口袋,触碰到了三根绿色的鹦鹉羽毛。

他深吸了一口气,踏上最上面的一层石阶。"我要下去!"他说。

丁丁摸着墙上冰冷的石头走下台阶。他尽力不去想潮湿洞穴里挂着的黏糊糊的东西。

接着，他的一只手摸到了一个方形的硬东西。是电灯开关！他向上拨动，整个空间突然灯火通明。

"原来是一条长长的隧道！"他大喊。

露丝赶紧跑下石阶。她对乔希说："你要下来吗？"

"好吧。"乔希叹了口气，"但如果有什么东西碰到我，我就要离开这儿！"

狭窄的隧道里非常寒冷。他们沿着肮脏的地面一路往前走。头顶的岩壁上挂着结满蜘蛛网的小灯泡。空气中有股腐朽的气味。

隧道里有一段路很直，随后拐了一个弯。

"听，"露丝说，"我听见了水声。"

"我讨厌这里，"乔希说，"真的讨厌。"

丁丁拐弯后，发现自己正站在水里。有什么东西发出一声尖叫，丁丁被吓呆了。

乔希吓得搂住了丁丁的脖子。"到底是什么啊？"他尖叫着说。

"乔希，你勒着我了！"丁丁嘶哑着声音说。

"对不起。"乔希说。

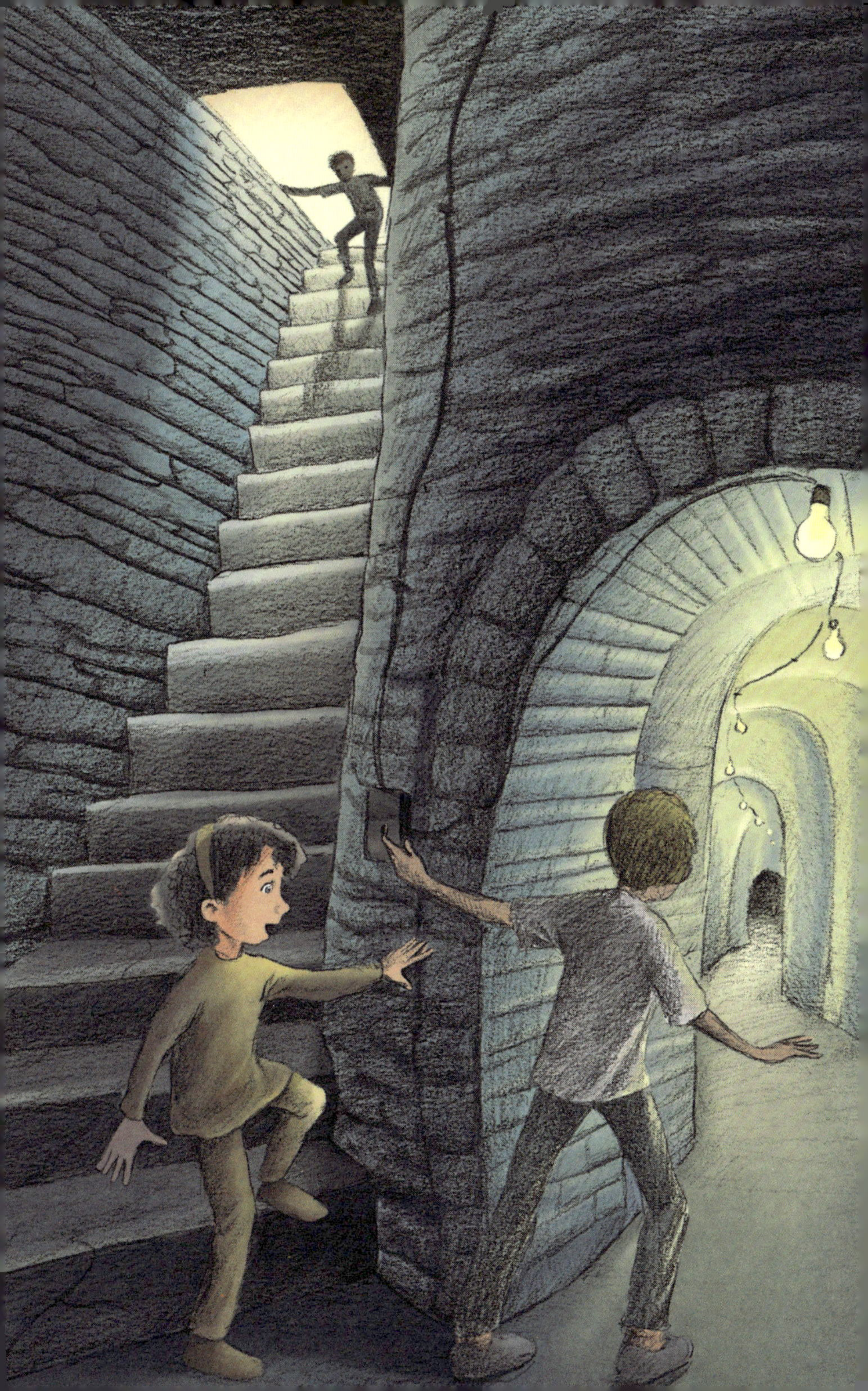

A to Z 神秘案件

"我们在哪儿?"露丝问。

他们正站在通往一个洞穴的入口。岩壁渗出了水,地面被淹没。左边另一条隧道向看不见的地方延伸。

"我想我知道我们在哪里。"丁丁小声说。

"我也知道!"乔希说,"我们在地牢里。但愿我不会看见骷髅!"

"如果昨天我们在洞穴内继续往前走,"丁丁接着说,"我们就会来到这里。"

"这是一条长长的隧道,"露丝说,"从游乐房一直通到大海!"

这时,他们身后传来一声响亮的尖叫。

乔希吓得跳了起来,差点把丁丁撞倒。

"你们看,"露丝说,"那边!"她指着墙边一个高高耸起的、黑乎乎的土堆。

丁丁蹚过冰冷的水快速走了过去,溅起一阵水花。

"是防水布。"他说。

丁丁屏住呼吸,抓住防水布的一角掀开。下面是两个笼子,一个在上,一个在下。每个笼子

恐怖的地牢

里有四只绿色的大鹦鹉。

鹦鹉们吓坏了，翅膀用力地拍打着笼子的栅栏。尖叫声不停地在洞穴里回响。

"埃默里·斯科特的鬼魂就是这么回事。"露丝说。

乔希哈哈大笑："没错！如果撞到他的鬼魂，我都不知道我会做什么！"

丁丁从口袋里掏出羽毛，把它们放在一只鹦鹉旁边。

"一模一样。"他说。

"这到底是什么地方？"露丝问，"是谁把鹦鹉藏在了洞穴里？"

"我不知道。"丁丁说。

"伙伴们！"露丝看着地面说，"潮汐要来了，水越来越深了！"

丁丁和乔希低头看向地面，水已经没过了他们的脚踝！

"鹦鹉！"乔希说。

底下的笼子已经湿了。水势上涨，鹦鹉惊慌地尖叫起来。

63

"带它们出去!"丁丁说着,抓起上面的笼子,将它搬到隧道里干燥的地方。

乔希和露丝搬着另一个笼子。他们沿着隧道快速往回走,鹦鹉们害怕地尖叫。

丁丁停在最下面一级台阶那儿,抬头看了一眼:"噢,完蛋了!"

"怎么了?"露丝喘着气问。

"我记得我们没有关活板门。"丁丁说。

"是没有关啊。"乔希接话。

"但是,现在它关上了。"丁丁把笼子放在地上。他走上台阶推了推门。门纹丝不动。

乔希爬上台阶,两人一起推门。

"没用。"丁丁说,"一定是门掉下来,锁啪的一下关上了。"

"那怎么办?"露丝问,"如果潮汐淹没隧道……"

丁丁回到台阶下面:"还有一条路可以出去。但是我们得游泳。"

第十章

"哪条路?"露丝问。

"我们可以回到洞穴,从那条隧道游出去。"丁丁解释,"但是那里有蝙蝠!"

"那是唯一的出路。"乔希说。

孩子们搬着两个笼子回到隧道。鹦鹉们惊声尖叫,拍打着翅膀。

洞穴里的水差不多到他们的膝盖了,而且还在上涨。

"我们得尽快离开这儿。"乔希说。

露丝注视着另一条隧道。"不知道这儿离海滩有多远。"她说。

"不会很远,"丁丁说,"我们很可能就在城堡下面。"

"带着笼子怎么游泳呢?"乔希一边问,一边环顾漆黑的洞穴,"我们需要一个木筏或类似的东西。"

"如果水还不太深,我们可以走出去。"丁丁说。

他把笼子递给露丝,然后走进更深的水里。水到了他的腰间。

"这水有点冷,"他颤抖着说,"但还不是那么深。我们可以把笼子拿出去。"

"如果水越来越深呢?"乔希说,"我们不可能把笼子放在头顶!"

"我有办法!"露丝说,"我在《女童子军》杂志上看过一篇文章,那上面有介绍如何用牛仔裤当漂浮物——在脚踝处和裤腿处打结,裤子充气后就可以做成浮水圈。"

"你的意思是脱下裤子?"乔希说,"没门儿!"

恐怖的地牢

"好主意!"丁丁说。他从深水里出来,脱下鞋子和湿牛仔裤。给牛仔裤裤腿打完结,他又穿好鞋子。

丁丁看着乔希。"快点,"他说,"水越来越深了。"

"好吧,不过我觉得这样很别扭。"乔希咕哝着,脱下鞋子和牛仔裤。水刚好到了平角短裤下面。

丁丁给乔希的裤腿也打好结,把两条裤子放入水中。充满空气的牛仔裤漂浮起来了!

"准备好了吗?"丁丁说。他们走入水里,让两个笼子在漂浮的牛仔裤上保持平衡。

"这办法有用!"露丝说。

"这水又冷又臭。"乔希说。

"至少还能触到地。"丁丁说,"好了,走吧。"

他们蹚水离开洞穴时,隧道里越来越黑暗。水已经没过了他们的胸部,所幸没有继续上涨。

鹦鹉们一路都很安静,似乎知道自己获救了。

"你觉得水里有鲨鱼吗?"乔希问。他的声

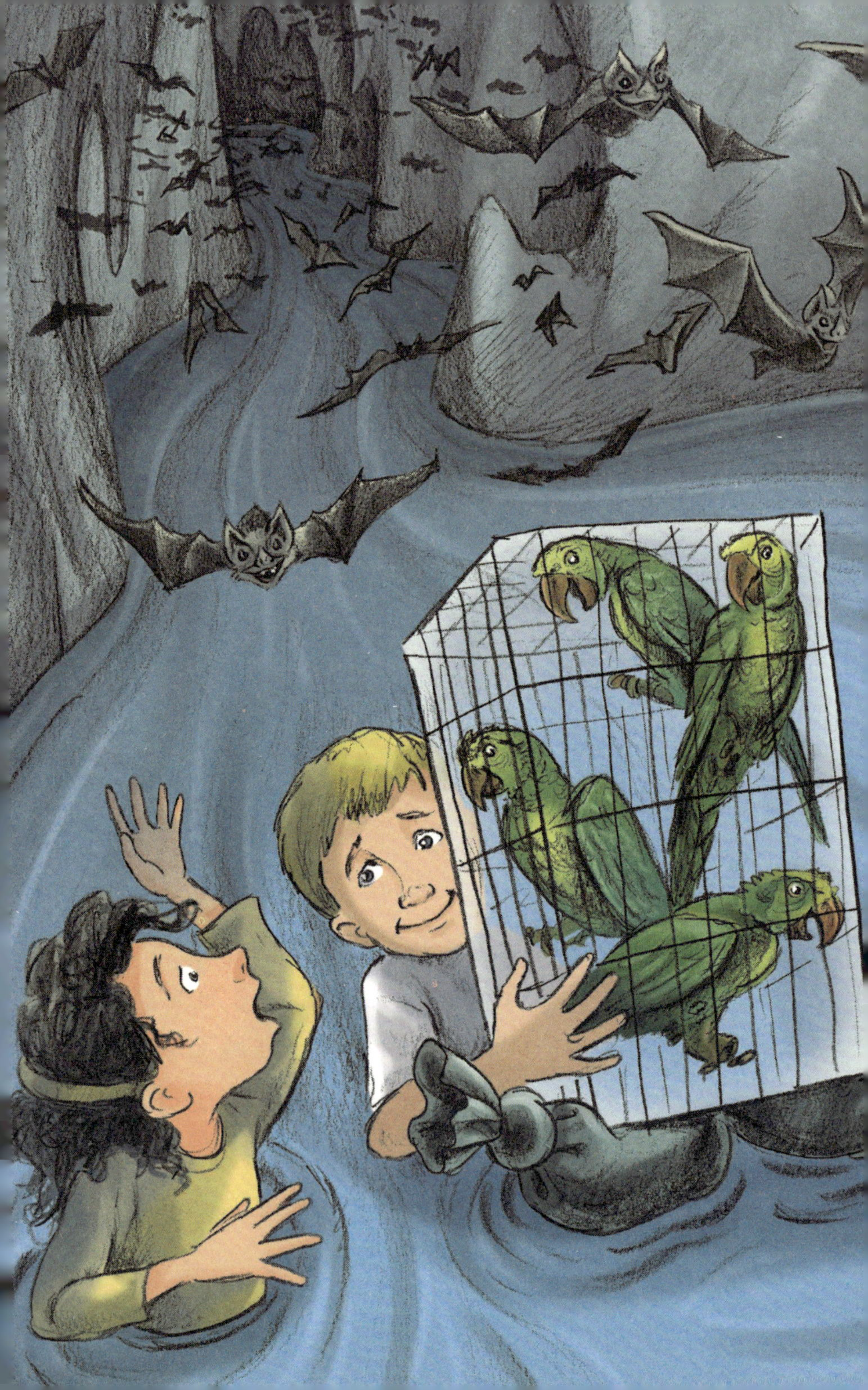

音在洞中回荡。

"没有。"丁丁说,"只有一些吃人的龙虾。"

突然,他们听见黑暗中传来沙沙的声音。

"什么声音?"露丝问。

"冷静。"乔希咯咯地笑着说,"是蝙蝠。一定是我们吓着它们了。"

"蝙蝠友好吗?"露丝问。

A to Z 神秘案件

"如果你是一只昆虫，它们可不友好。"乔希回答。他们终于看见日光了，前方就是隧道的尽头——大海。

"我们成功了，伙伴们！"丁丁说道。他们把笼子和湿透的牛仔裤拖到之前野餐的海滩上。

"伙伴们，晒着太阳很舒服吧！"乔希说着，扑通一声躺在沙滩上。

孩子们休息了一会儿后，平复了呼吸。丁丁和乔希解开牛仔裤的结，将牛仔裤铺开晾干。

"这些鹦鹉，"乔希说，"我在一本讲濒危鸟类的书上见过。"

"为什么有人把濒危的鹦鹉藏在洞穴里？"露丝问。

"盗猎者。"乔希说着，脱下湿透的鞋子，"盗猎者捕捉稀有动物，将它们卖掉可以得到一大笔钱。"

"是谁呢？"

乔希耸了耸肩："知道这条隧道的人。"

"我知道是谁了。"丁丁说。

乔西和露丝看着他。

"谁?"乔希问。

丁丁面露悲伤:"沃克·华莱士。"

第十一章

"什么?"露丝大声说,"难以置信!"

丁丁耸了耸肩:"我在他的吉普车里和船上分别发现了一根羽毛。"

乔希缓慢地点了点头:"还有昨天我们在这儿野餐时,沃利斯说沃克进了洞穴。或许他发现了游乐房的活板门。"

"地毯上的脚印那么大,就是他的。"丁丁说道。

露丝站起来,掸掉湿牛仔裤上的沙子:"我不相信你们俩说的。沃克不会违法的！而且他绝不会利用他妹妹的房子干坏事！"

"但愿不是他。"丁丁说，"无论如何，我们要把鹦鹉带回城堡！"

丁丁和乔希穿上湿淋淋的牛仔裤，抱起笼子。几分钟后他们来到了沃利斯的厨房。

她正在桌旁写作。

"我们查出是什么发出怪叫声了！"丁丁脱口而出。

孩子们和沃利斯说了通往洞穴的那条隧道和有关鹦鹉的事。

"游乐房里竟然有一扇活板门！"沃利斯睁大双眼，惊讶地说，"还有一条隧道？真是不可思议啊！"

"像是一条秘密通道。"乔希说，"也许海盗们把金子藏在那儿了！"

"哦，我不知道什么海盗。"沃利斯说，"但我现在知道埃默里·斯科特是如何把大理石之类的东西运到这上面来的了！"

"我们该怎么处理这些鹦鹉呢？"露丝问。

"让我看看。"沃利斯说。

他们一起来到换鞋室。门一开,鹦鹉们在笼子里扑扇着翅膀。尖叫声充斥着整个房间。

"可怜的鸟儿。"沃利斯说,"喂它们吃点东西吧?鹦鹉吃什么?"

"有水果吗?"乔希说,"它们在热带雨林就吃水果。"

沃利斯向厨房走去。

"不知道这些鹦鹉来自哪儿?"露丝说。

乔希仔细观察鹦鹉。"可能来自非洲或者南美洲。"他说。

"盗猎者是怎么把它们带来缅因州的?"丁丁问道。

"用船啊。"乔希说,"再用小一号的船带到洞穴里面。"

"像沃克那样的小船——"

丁丁没有再说下去,因为沃利斯过来了,拿着两根剥好的香蕉和一串葡萄。他们把水果放进笼子。鹦鹉们用喙啄着水果。

"它们快饿死了!"沃利斯说着,在每个笼子里放了一碗水。

"我也饿了。"乔希说,"我们没吃午餐。"

"噢,那可不行!"沃利斯说,"去厨房吃点东西。"

沃利斯做三明治时,丁丁说起前一天晚上他看见的树林里的光:"我敢说还有更多装着鹦鹉的笼子。那些人晚上通过游乐房把鹦鹉运出去。"

"我们应该藏在树林里,看看是谁在做坏事!"露丝说。

沃利斯摇了摇头:"绝对不行。那些人是很危险的!"

她拿出盘子和餐巾纸:"今天是周日,明天上午我打电话给州议会厅。他们一定有专门负责对付盗猎者的工作人员。"

沃利斯看着孩子们:"答应我,别再去那条隧道和那个洞穴了。"

丁丁在桌子下面用脚踢了踢露丝和乔希。

"我们答应你。"他说。

午餐后,孩子们回到游乐房。他们清洗了餐具,清理了地毯。

"我希望我们能抓住那些盗猎者。"丁丁说。

"我认为我们应该睡在游乐房,"乔希说,"然后谁来了,我们就抓住谁!"

"乔希,他们会把我们抓住并关进笼子。"露丝说。

"而且沃利斯也不会同意我们睡在这里的。"丁丁说,"但我还有一个主意。"

凌晨一点半,在丁丁和乔希黑暗的卧室里,孩子们穿戴整齐,蹲在窗户边。

乔希打着哈欠说:"今晚可能不会有人来。"

"也许他们知道笼子被我们发现了,"丁丁说,"沃克可能在他的小船上看见我们了。"

"我还是不相信是沃克做的。"露丝说,"但不管是谁,都要来喂鹦鹉,对吧?"

"对。"丁丁说,"我们轮流监视吧。我先来,你们俩可以眯一会儿。"

"如果看见坏人,你就叫醒我!"乔希说着,上了床。

"嗯,我不累。"露丝说,"希望这些坏人坐

恐怖的地牢

一百年牢！"

她和丁丁盯着茫茫的黑夜。时间随着闹钟的嘀嗒声流逝。

乔希打呼噜了。

"快看，"过了一会儿，露丝轻声说，"一只萤火虫。"

丁丁看见一点亮光缓慢地穿梭在黑暗中。"你叫醒乔希，"他对露丝说，"那不是萤火虫！"

三个孩子踮着脚经过沃利斯的卧室，匆匆下楼，从换鞋室出去。他们蹑手蹑脚地来到游乐房附近。

月光洒在空地上，一辆黑色汽车停在离游乐房几码[1]远的阴影处。

丁丁抓住乔希和露丝，向前方指了指。那是沃克的吉普车！

"看来你说对了。"露丝低声说，声音中透露出悲伤。

孩子们小步前行。突然，丁丁看见游乐房中

1.码：英美制长度单位。1码=0.9144米。——编者

77

透出一束光。

一名男子弯着腰，正在拉活板门！他的脚边放着一个亮着的手电筒。

男子站起身时，手电筒照到了他的脸，丁丁认出了这个人。

露丝抓住丁丁的手臂。"里普利·皮尔斯！"她轻声说。

不一会儿，里普走下台阶，进了隧道。

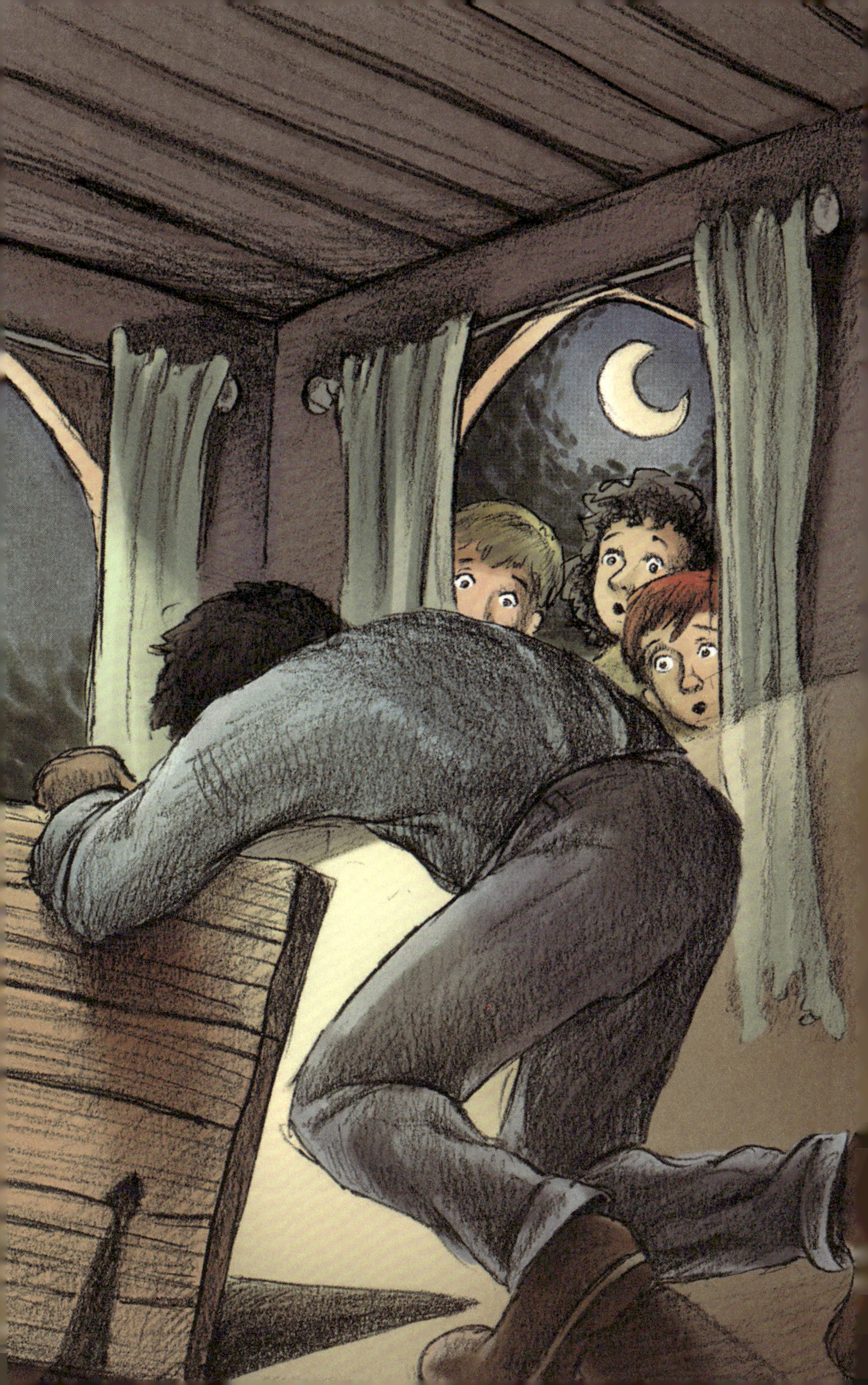

突然,乔希快速绕过游乐房的一角,从开着的门进去了。

丁丁还未来得及说话,乔希砰的一下就把活板门关上了。丁丁听见弹簧锁咔的一声锁住了。

第十二章

"反盗猎报警电话是什么?"第二天丁丁问。

"是800开头的电话号码,缅因州举报盗猎者的电话号码都是这样的。"沃利斯解释道。她又拿了一些热煎饼放到桌上。

大家昨晚几乎都没睡。锁上活板门后,丁丁、乔希和露丝跑回来叫醒了沃利斯。她拨打了报警电话,报告住宅地有盗猎者。

警察来了,逮捕了里普。警察给了沃利斯一个反盗猎报警电话。

然后沃利斯开着沃克的吉普车去了他家,把他接到了城堡来。

"缅因州渔猎部将好好盘问里普,"沃克说,"交易濒危动物是触犯联邦法律的。"

"里普是怎么得到那些鹦鹉的?"乔希问。

"他肯定跟能够抓到鹦鹉的国家的人有联系。"沃克说,"警察会调查他的电话记录,看他都跟谁联系了。"

"他很可能用自己的捕虾船运送鹦鹉。"沃利斯摇着头说,"难怪他的船总是那么干净。"

"他为什么用您的吉普车?"乔希问。

沃克又叉了一块煎饼:"里普的车前几天坏了,所以我把车借给他用。"

"多完美的计划啊。"沃利斯说,"里普需要钱,他已经联系好了愿意花重金购买珍稀鹦鹉的人。"

"不知道他是否还卖过其他动物。"乔希说,"比如猴子或蛇。"

"我们以后会知道的。"沃克说着,朝乔希眨了眨眼,"你怎么会想到关上活板门,把里普关

在里面?"

"我很生气!"乔希答道,"就想让他体会一下被关在笼子里的感觉。"

"所以乔希鞋子上粘到的绿色羽毛就是从里普那儿来的,对吗?"丁丁问。

沃克点点头:"很可能是他的鞋子粘到了羽毛,带到了吉普车上。你在我船上捡到的那根羽毛同样如此。"

乔希的脸红了。"我们一度以为您是盗猎者呢。"他对沃克说。

"哼,我可从来没这样以为!"露丝说。沃克笑着对露丝说:"谢谢你!你怎么确信不是我呢?"

"你很忙。"她说,"而且你才不会虐待鹦鹉呢。昨天你把小螃蟹都扔回海里了。"

"那些鹦鹉会被怎么处理?"丁丁问。

"我认为它们会被送回原所在地。"沃克说,"里普则很可能会坐牢。"

"多亏了你们三个,我再也不会听见怪异的响声了。"沃利斯说。

她不好意思地笑了:"但说实话,我想我会想

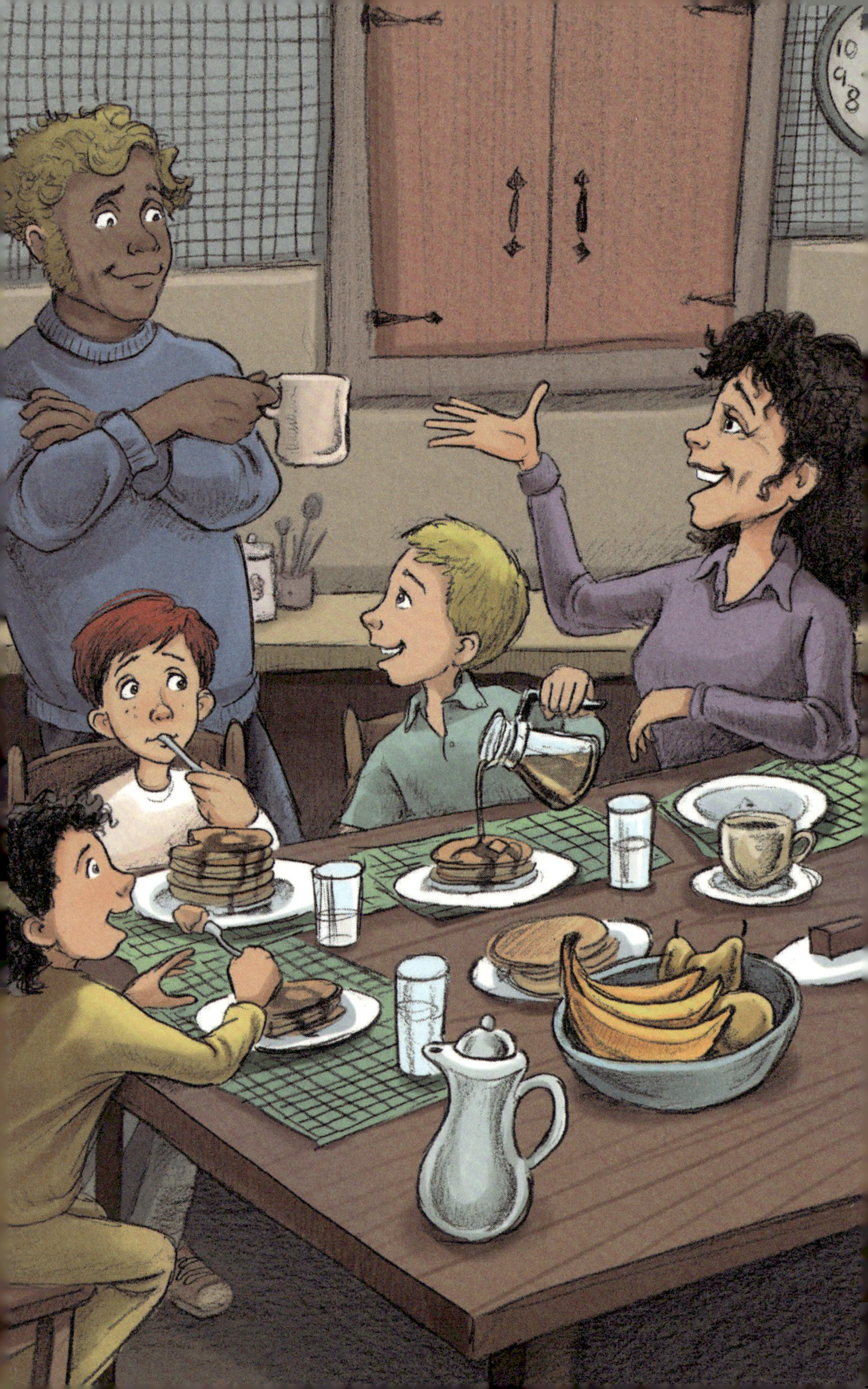

念埃默里·斯科特的鬼魂的。我有点喜欢住在一座闹鬼的城堡里呢!"

就在这时,一声尖叫从换鞋室传来。

A to Z Mysteries®

The Deadly Dungeon

by Ron Roy

illustrated by
John Steven Gurney

BELFAST, MAINE
GREEN LAWN
N
W
E
S
SIDE DOOR
PLAYHOUSE
PATH TO PLAYHOUSE
ROAD TO BELFAST, MAINE

Welcome to A to Z Mysteries
on Location
at Moose Manor
ATLANTIC
OCEAN
MOAT
GARDEN
CASTLE
STEPS
TO
BEACH
MOAT
FRONT
DOOR
DRAWBRIDGE
PICNIC
BEACH

Chapter 1

Dink squirmed in his seat. He, Josh, and Ruth Rose had been riding the bus since seven that morning.

They were on their way to Maine to visit their friend Wallis Wallace, a famous mystery writer. The three of them had met her when she came to Green Lawn. Dink smiled when he remembered how they had rescued Wallis from a "kidnapper."

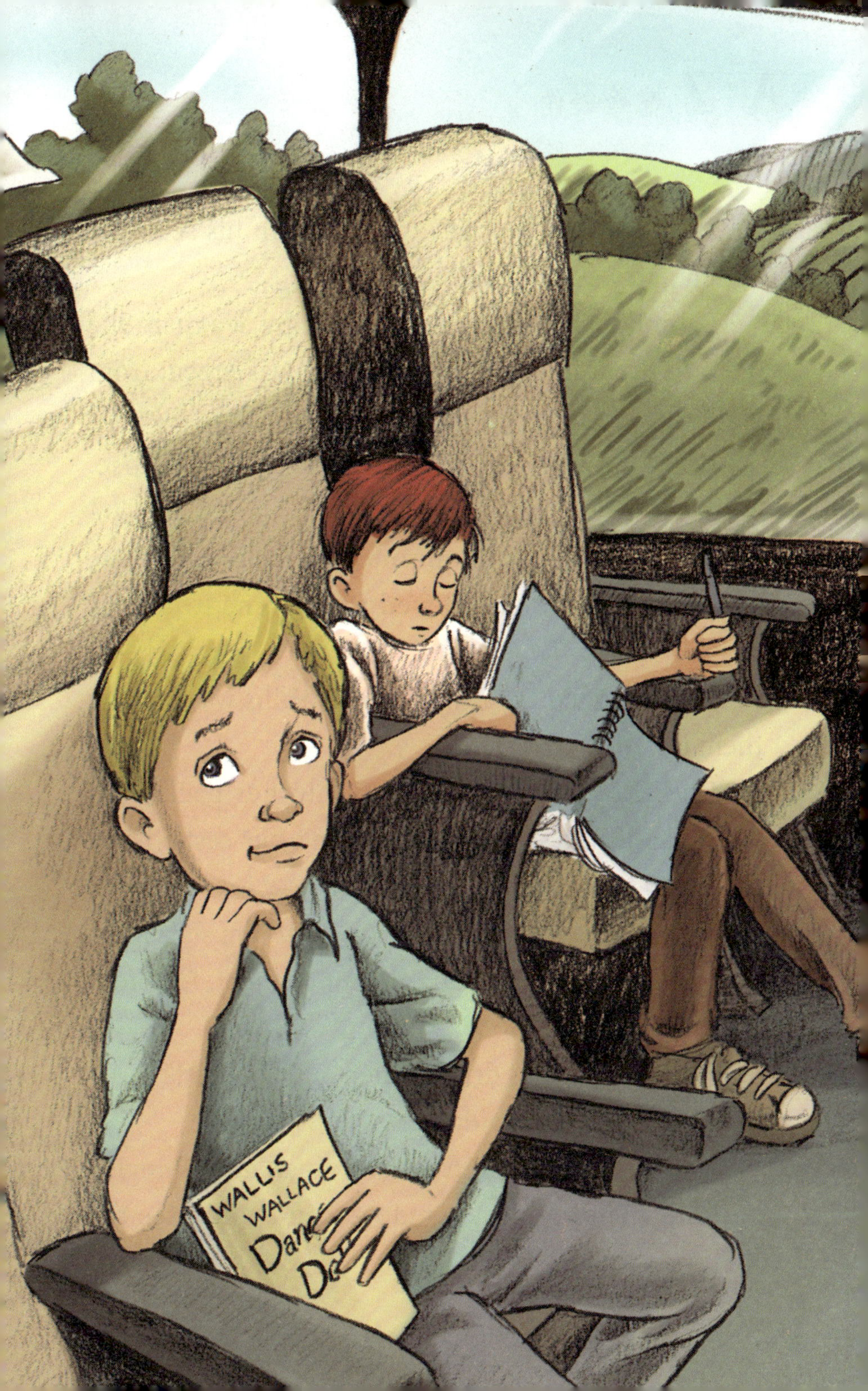
WALLIS
WALLACE

Dink glanced over at Josh, asleep in his seat. His sketch pad was open on his lap.

Behind Josh, Ruth Rose was looking at a map. She liked to dress in one color. Today it was green, from her T-shirt to her high-tops.

Dink moved into the seat next to Ruth Rose. "Where are we?" he asked.

"Almost there." She pointed to Belfast, Maine, on her map. "We just passed a Welcome to Belfast sign."

Dink nodded. That was where Wallis was picking them up.

Ruth Rose tucked her map into her pack. "I'm so excited!" she said. "Do you think her castle has a moat and a dungeon?"

"I just hope it has food," Dink said. "I'm starving!"

Josh's head popped up in front of them. "Me too! Are we there yet?"

Just then the bus driver called out, "Belfast!"

"All right!" Josh said, leaping into the aisle.

The bus stopped in front of a small gray-shingled building. Through the window, Dink could see the

恐怖的地牢

water.

"Do you see Wallis?" Ruth Rose asked.

Dink grabbed his pack. "No, but let's get off. I think I'm allergic to buses!"

The kids headed for the front. They followed an elderly couple down the steps.

They were squinting into the blinding sunlight when they heard someone say, "Hi, kids!" A tall man with curly blond hair was walking toward them. His face was tanned and smiling.

"I remember you. You're Wallis's brother!" Ruth Rose said.

"Call me Walker, okay?" said the man. "Wallis is buying groceries, so she asked me to get you."

Walker Wallace picked up Dink's pack. It clunked heavily against his leg.

"What's in here, your rock collection?" he asked.

Dink grinned. "Books. My mom said it rains a lot in Maine, so I came prepared."

Walker laughed. "We've planned perfect weather for you guys. Sun every day! Come on, that's my Jeep over there."

Walker's dusty brown Jeep had no top. The leather seats were worn and split in places.

He swept a pair of boots and a tool belt onto the floor, making room in the backseat. "Pile in!"

The boys climbed into the back. Ruth Rose sat next to Walker. "How far is the castle?" she asked.

"Not far." Walker pointed. "About a mile past those trees."

He drove up the coast. "You guys hungry? Sis is buying everything in the store for you."

"I'm always hungry," Josh said, leaning back and crossing his legs. He took a deep breath of the ocean air. "What a smell!"

"I'll say," Dink said. "Get your smelly foot out of my face!"

"It's not smelly," Josh said, wiggling his sneaker under Dink's nose.

"What's this?" Dink plucked a bright green feather off the sole of Josh's sneaker.

Josh shrugged. "I must've picked it up on the bus."

Dink slipped the feather into his pocket.

"There's Moose Manor!" Walker called. He pointed through the trees.

Dink stared at the tall castle. It was built of huge gray stones. Its small dark windows looked like watching eyes. An iron fence surrounded the building.

"Cool," Dink said softly.

"Look, guys, a moat!" Ruth Rose said.

"And a drawbridge!" cried Josh.

Walker pulled up in front of the gate. The kids hopped out with their packs.

"I have to get back to my boat," Walker said. "Sis should be here soon. Have fun!" He waved and sped back through the trees.

Up close, the castle towered over the kids. The battlements on top reminded Dink of giant's teeth.

Josh pushed the gate, and it creaked open. They peered down into the moat. Ruth Rose let out a laugh. "Look, guys!"

The bottom of the empty moat was planted with flowers!

"Hey, guys!" Josh called. "Check this out!" He had crossed the drawbridge and was standing in front of an enormous wooden door. He tugged on the handle, but the door wouldn't budge. "How the heck does Wallis get in?"

Just then Dink heard a car. A red Volkswagen convertible zoomed up to the gate. The horn tooted, and a hand waved wildly.

"It's Wallis!" shouted Dink.

Chapter 2

"Welcome!" Wallis yelled.

She looked the same as Dink remembered: happy smile, curly brown hair, mischievous eyes.

"What do you think of Moose Manor?" she asked. "Isn't it fun?"

"I love it!" said Ruth Rose.

"It's awesome!" Josh said.

Wallis laughed. "It is something, isn't it? Help me with these groceries, and I'll take you on the grand tour!"

恐怖的地牢

The entrance to the castle turned out to be a regular-sized door around the corner. Wallis and the kids carried bags of groceries into a large room. Dink saw a washer and dryer, wooden pegs for hats and coats, and a pile of sneakers and boots.

"This is my mud room," Wallis said. "The kitchen is through here." She shoved open another door with her hip.

Dink had to tip his head back to see the high ceiling. The usual kitchen stuff was there, with a long wooden table in the middle. A black chandelier hung over the table.

"This place is humongous!" Dink said.

"That's why I love it," Wallis said. "Let's put the food away and I'll show you around."

The kids quickly emptied the bags while Wallis put the milk and ice cream into the refrigerator.

"Okay, the tour begins in the royal living room," Wallis said. "Follow me!" She led them into the biggest living room Dink had ever seen.

The first thing Dink noticed was the chandelier hanging right over his head. It was as big as Wallis's

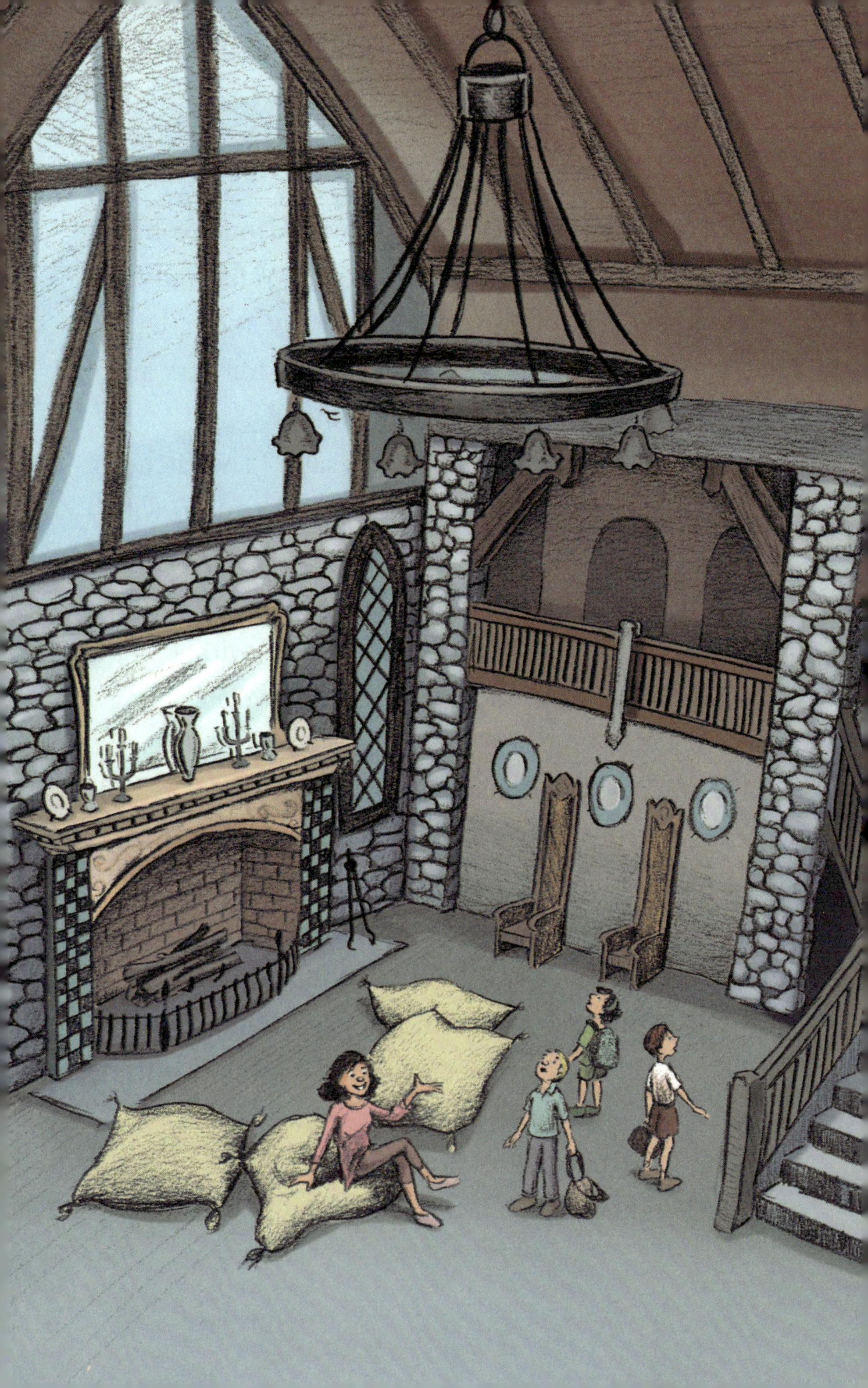

car!

A marble fireplace took up almost one whole wall. The mantel was dark wood, carved with all kinds of animals.

"This place is amazing!" Dink said.

"Geez," Josh breathed, peering into the fireplace. "You could burn a whole tree in here!"

Wallis flopped onto a pile of floor cushions. "Some winter days I wish I could," she said. "It gets mighty cold up on this cliff."

"How old is this place?" Ruth Rose asked, peering up at the tall stone walls.

"Pretty old," Wallis said. "It was built in the 1930s by a movie star named Emory Scott."

"Awesome!" Josh said.

"What happened to him?" Dink asked.

"Well…" Wallis raised her eyebrows and lowered her voice. "According to the town gossip, he died suddenly. Right here in the castle. In fact, sometimes I think I hear his ghost!"

The kids stared with open mouths.

Then Dink laughed. "Come on, you're just

kidding, right?"

"Why? Don't you believe in ghosts?" Wallis asked with a grin.

"No way!" they all yelled.

"Well…" Wallis stood up. "Maybe Emory will introduce himself when he's ready. In the meantime, why don't I show you your rooms?"

The kids grabbed their packs and followed Wallis up a wide stone stair-case to the second floor. At the top of the stairs was a dim hallway with several doors.

Wallis pointed to one. "That's my room. Ruth Rose, yours is there, and I've put you boys together, right across the hall."

Wallis tapped on a narrow door at the end of the hall. "This one leads up to the roof."

Dink opened the door to their bedroom. Like the rooms downstairs, the ceiling was high. A blue carpet covered the stone floor. The twin beds had bright red covers.

Dink went to the window and looked outside. All he could see were pine trees. "Where's the ocean?" he asked.

"On the other side," Wallis said. "Why don't you settle in, then come down for lunch?"

Ruth Rose went to her room. Dink and Josh dumped their packs on their beds.

"This place is so cool," Josh said, wandering into their bathroom.

Dink stacked his books on the table next to his bed. He pawed through his clothes, then changed into shorts and a T-shirt.

"Dink, come in here!" Josh called.

Dink wandered into the bathroom.

"Listen," Josh said. He had his ear against one of the bathroom walls.

"What're you doing?" asked Dink.

Josh made a shushing sound. "I thought I heard something!"

"What's going on?" Ruth Rose said as she came into the room.

"Josh thought he heard something behind the wall," Dink said.

Ruth Rose grinned. "It must be the ghost of Emory Scott. He's just waiting for you two to fall

103

asleep tonight!"

Just then they heard Wallis's voice. "Come and get it!" she called. They raced down to the kitchen.

Wallis was packing a basket. "It's such a great day, I thought we'd have a picnic on the beach," she said.

"Cool!" Josh said. "Can we go fishing there sometime?"

Wallis nodded. "Ask Walker if you can borrow some gear. In fact, he's taking you lobstering tomorrow."

"Awesome!" Josh yelled.

Wallis smiled. "You won't think so at four-thirty tomorrow morning."

Dink and Josh each grabbed one end of the picnic basket. Wallis handed Ruth Rose a blanket, then led them to the back of the castle and through another gate.

"Great view, isn't it?" Wallis said. "The first time I saw this place, I knew I had to do my writing here."

Dink took a deep breath of the sea air. Small boats made colorful dots against the blue ocean. "It's really nice," he said.

Josh peered nervously over the cliff. "How do we

恐怖的地牢

get down?"

Wallis laughed. "See there? I had steps built. But poor Emory Scott! You remember that marble fireplace and that massive chandelier? Every piece came from Europe by boat. Goodness knows how he got them up this cliff!"

Suddenly a scream burst from the castle behind them.

Dink nearly dropped his end of the picnic basket. The skin on his arms erupted into a thousand goose bumps.

Wallis glanced back and grinned. "Dink, Josh, Ruth Rose, allow me to introduce…the ghost of Emory Scott!"

Chapter 3

The kids stared at Wallis in silence.

She winked at them. "Don't worry, that's just his way of saying hello. Shall we go down?"

The kids glanced at each other, then followed Wallis down the wooden stairs. At the bottom they found a small, sandy beach.

Dink and Josh set the basket in the shade of some boulders while Wallis and Ruth Rose spread the blanket.

"Look! A cave!" Josh said, pointing at a tunnel at the bottom of the cliff. The sea snaked into the dark hole, making a narrow river.

"How far does it go in?" Josh asked, peering into the black space.

"I don't know," Wallis said. "Walker told me that it's full of bats."

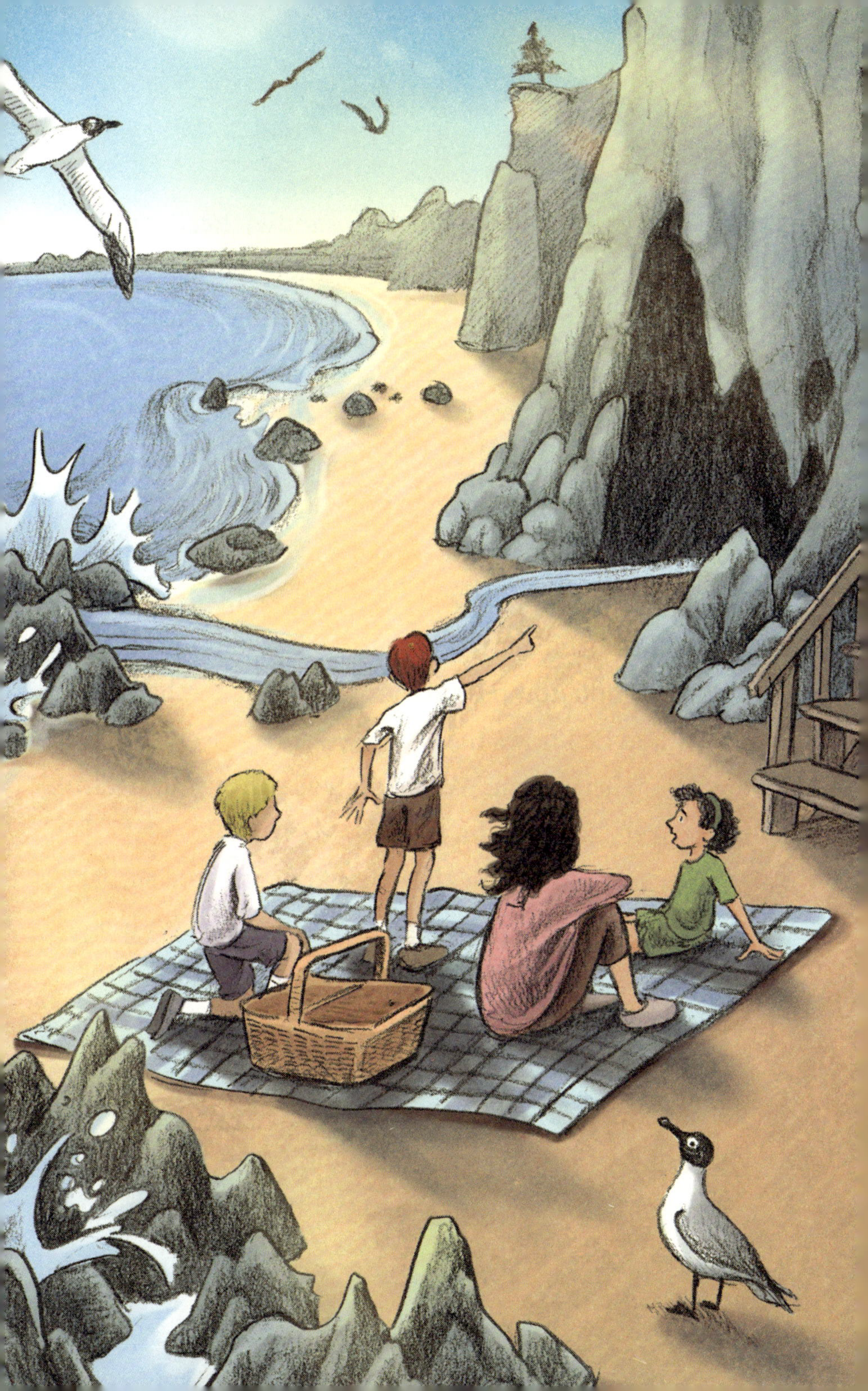

They picnicked on chicken sandwiches, apples, chocolate chip cookies, and cold lemonade. Wallis pointed down the shoreline. "Walker's house is beyond those trees."

"Where is he?" asked Dink.

"Out on his boat," Wallis said, waving a cookie at the ocean. "His lobster pots are scattered over about a half mile of very deep water."

"How does he find them?" Josh asked.

Wallis wiped her fingers on a paper napkin. "Well, he has a good compass aboard Lady Luck—that's his boat—and he knows the water."

After their picnic, Wallis put everything back into the basket. "Ready for a walk?"

They hiked along the rocky beach. Ruth Rose poked into tide pools and picked up shells. Josh hung his sneakers around his neck and waded along the shore.

"Better watch out for lobsters," Dink teased. "They like smelly toes."

Josh grinned and splashed Dink.

Rounding a curve in the shoreline, Wallis pointed.

"There's Walker's place."

It was a gray cottage with a red roof, surrounded by dune grass and sand.

Just then they heard a shout. Dink looked around and saw someone waving from the end of a dock.

Wallis waved back. "Kids, come and meet our friend Ripley Pearce."

They walked out on the dock toward a long green boat tied at the end. The boat's brass and wood trim gleamed in the sunlight.

A man stood next to the boat, holding a dripping sponge. He had dark slicked-back hair and blue eyes.

"Hi, Rip," Wallis said. "Meet Dink Duncan, Josh Pinto, and Ruth Rose Hathaway."

The man smiled and stuck out a hand. He had dazzling white teeth and a deep tan. "You're fans of this lady's books, right?"

"I've got all of them!" Dink announced.

"I met these three in Connecticut," Wallis explained. "They're spending a week up at the castle. Why don't you come for supper with us tonight?"

"I like your boat," Ruth Rose said. "It's so shiny

and clean!"

Rip flashed her a grin. "Thank you very much, little lady. I'll see you tonight at dinner."

Then he looked at Josh. "Want to untie me?" he asked, pointing to a rope tied to the end of the dock.

Josh untied the rope and handed it to Rip.

"Nice meeting you kids," he said, stepping aboard his boat. He started the engine, and the boat pulled smoothly away from the dock.

Dink watched the boat cut through the water. "Maybe I won't be a writer when I grow up. Maybe I'll get a lobster boat."

Wallis grinned at Dink. "Better stick to writing, Dink. Lobsters are getting scarce in Maine."

"I can't wait to go out on Walker's boat," Ruth Rose said.

"My brother's boat is nothing like Rip's," Wallis said. She shook her head. "I don't know how Rip keeps his so clean. Walker's boat looks and smells like a lobster boat."

They walked back toward their picnic spot. Josh kicked water on Ruth Rose, and she chased him down the beach, yelling all the way.

Dink walked quietly along with Wallis. Overhead, a sea gull cried out.

Dink looked up at Wallis. "Do you really think that scream we heard was the ghost of Emory Scott?"

Wallis laughed. "All I know is I've been hearing those screams since I moved in. The first time, I searched the castle. But I never found a thing."

Dink shivered. "Do you hear the noises a lot?" he asked.

Wallis shrugged. "Sometimes weeks go by and there's not a peep. Then I'll hear them for a few days in a row."

Wallis smiled down at Dink. "To tell you the truth, Dink, this is one mystery that's got me stumped. If those screams aren't the ghost of Emory Scott, I don't know what they are!"

Chapter 4

At the top of the cliff, Wallis took the picnic things. "I need to spend sometime working on my new book," she said. "Why don't you guys go exploring? Emory Scott built a playhouse for his kids in those trees. You might want to check it out."

She opened the side door. "Oh, I almost forgot," she said with twinkling eyes. "Some people think his ghost hangs around there, looking for his children. So keep your eyes open!" With that, she went inside.

The kids found a path through the trees. As they

walked, Dink told Josh and Ruth Rose what Wallis had said on the beach.

"So it is a ghost!" Josh said. "Creepy!"

"No way," Ruth Rose said. "I don't believe in ghosts. It must be an animal trapped somewhere in the castle."

"I don't know," Dink said. "Wallis told me she searched the whole place."

"Besides," said Josh, "what kind of animal makes a spooky scream like that?"

Just then the kids reached the playhouse. The outside of the small wooden building had been painted to look like Wallis's castle. A kid-sized drawbridge crossed a shallow moat to the front door.

"Excellent," said Josh.

"Let's go inside!" Ruth Rose cried, running to the door. She tugged on the handle, and the door opened with a soft whoosh.

Ruth Rose curtsied. "Enter, my loyal knights!"

"His Highness King Dink goes first," Dink said, nudging ahead of Josh.

They crowded into the room. Everything was

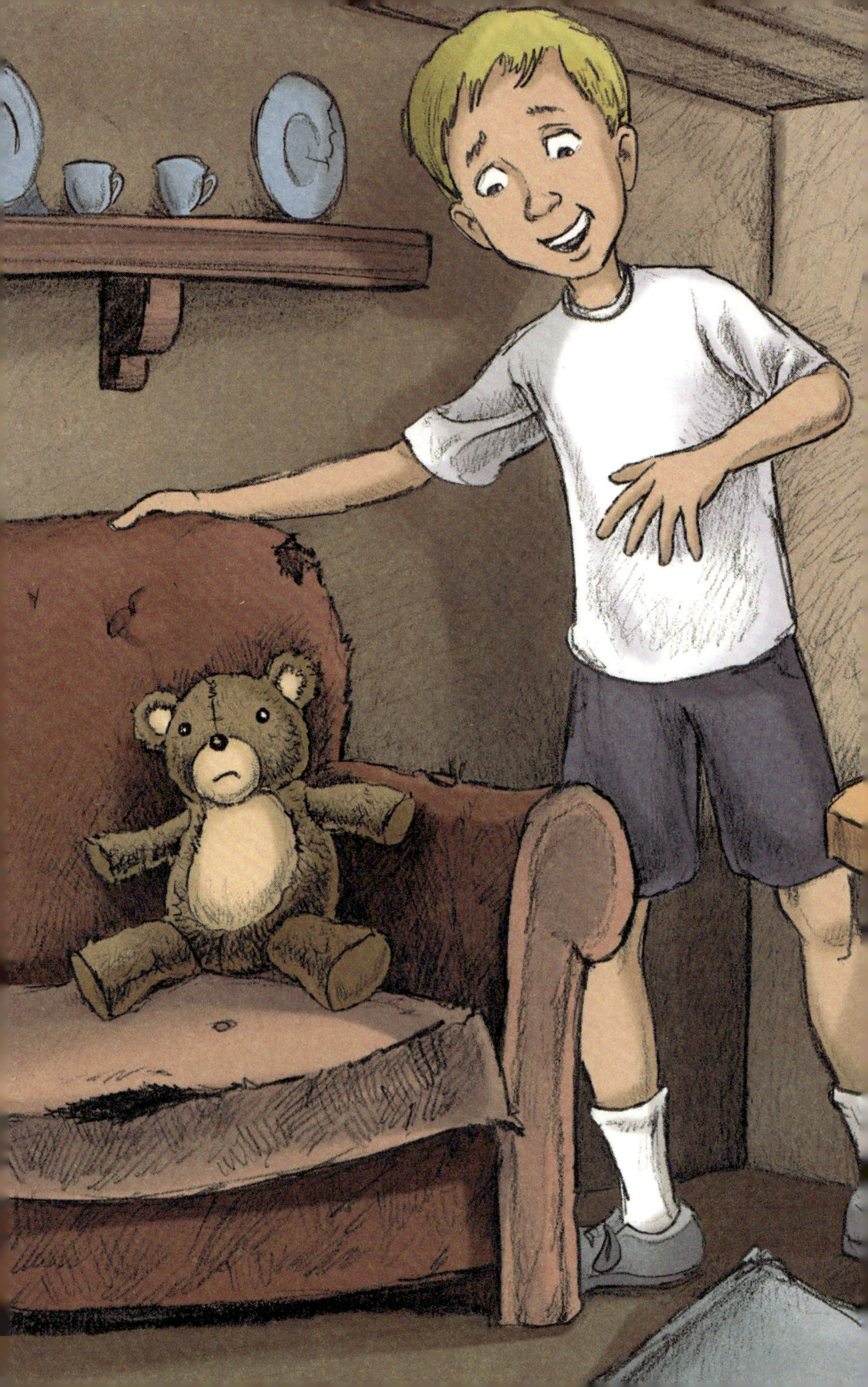

covered with a layer of dust. Dim light shone through two small windows covered with cobwebs.

Josh rubbed his arms. "Boy, this place is cold," he said.

"Looks like no one's been in here for years," Ruth Rose said.

A round table and two little chairs stood in the middle of the room on a dusty, worn rug. A shelf held a miniature set of blue dishes. Under the shelf, a lonely-looking teddy bear sat on an old sofa.

"This place creeps me out," Josh said.

"Look," Dink said. "Footprints on the rug." He stepped into one of them. "Whoever made these sure has big feet!"

"Do ghosts leave footprints?" Josh asked.

"Maybe it's Walker," Ruth Rose suggested. "They're too big to be Wallis's."

"But why would Walker come here?" Dink wondered out loud.

"Can we go?" Josh pleaded. "I just saw a monster spider, and he was looking back at me!"

"Okay, but let's come back," Ruth Rose said. "I want to clean this place. It's sad to see it all dusty like this."

Ruth Rose pulled the door shut behind them. As they crossed the drawbridge, Dink noticed something in the moat. He jumped down and picked up a bright green feather.

"Hey, guys, look! It's like the one that was stuck to Josh's sneaker."

Ruth Rose held the feather up to the sun. "What's it from?"

Josh examined the feather. "The only bird I know with this kind of feather is a parrot," he said. "But parrots don't live in Maine."

Dink took the feather back from Josh, then put it in his pocket.

"Okay, we've explored the playhouse," Josh said. "Now you guys have to do what I want."

Dink grinned at his friend. "You mean eat?"

"No. I want to check out that cave down on the beach."

"Wait a minute," Dink said. "You were creeped out by the playhouse, but you want to explore the cave?"

"Caves are cool," Josh said. "Come on, you guys."

The kids headed past the castle, through the gate, and down the cliff. They stood looking at the small river flowing out of the cave. "I wonder how deep it is," Dink said.

"There's one way to find out," Josh said. He stepped in the water and began wading into the cave. The water reached just above his ankles.

117

"Come on, you guys!" he called over his shoulder.

Dink and Ruth Rose followed him. The cave grew darker, until the sunlight disappeared. The air was cold and damp, and the black walls felt slimy.

"Josh, this water is freezing," Ruth Rose said. Her voice sounded hollow. "I hate it in here! Can we go back?"

"The water's getting deeper, too," Dink said. "And I can't even see you guys!"

"Shh!" Josh said. "I heard something!"

"Josh, don't try to scare us!" Ruth Rose said. "I'm already—"

Suddenly a scream echoed through the cave.

"RUN!" Ruth Rose yelled.

Over their heads, hundreds of black bats streaked for daylight.

Chapter 5

The kids didn't stop running till they were at the top of the cliff. Dink threw himself on the ground, trying to catch his breath.

"What was that?" Ruth Rose asked, pulling off her sopping sneakers. "My heart nearly stopped!"

"It was the ghost!" Josh said. "I bet that cave leads to a secret dungeon under the castle. Maybe that's where Emory Scott died!"

Ruth Rose burst out laughing. Josh ignored her. "There must be a secret door leading to the dungeon somewhere. And I'm going to find it!"

"Maybe you are," Dink said. "But I'm gonna take a shower and change."

"Me too," Ruth Rose said. "I smell like a fish!"

When they got back to the castle, Walker's Jeep was parked out front. The kids cleaned up, then hurried down to the kitchen. Wallis, Walker and Rip were sitting at the long table, husking ears of corn.

"Hi, kids," Walker said. "How was your first day at Moose Manor?"

"It was great," Josh said, shooting Dink a look. "We explored the playhouse and found some neat stuff on the beach."

Dink figured Josh wanted to keep his "secret dungeon"

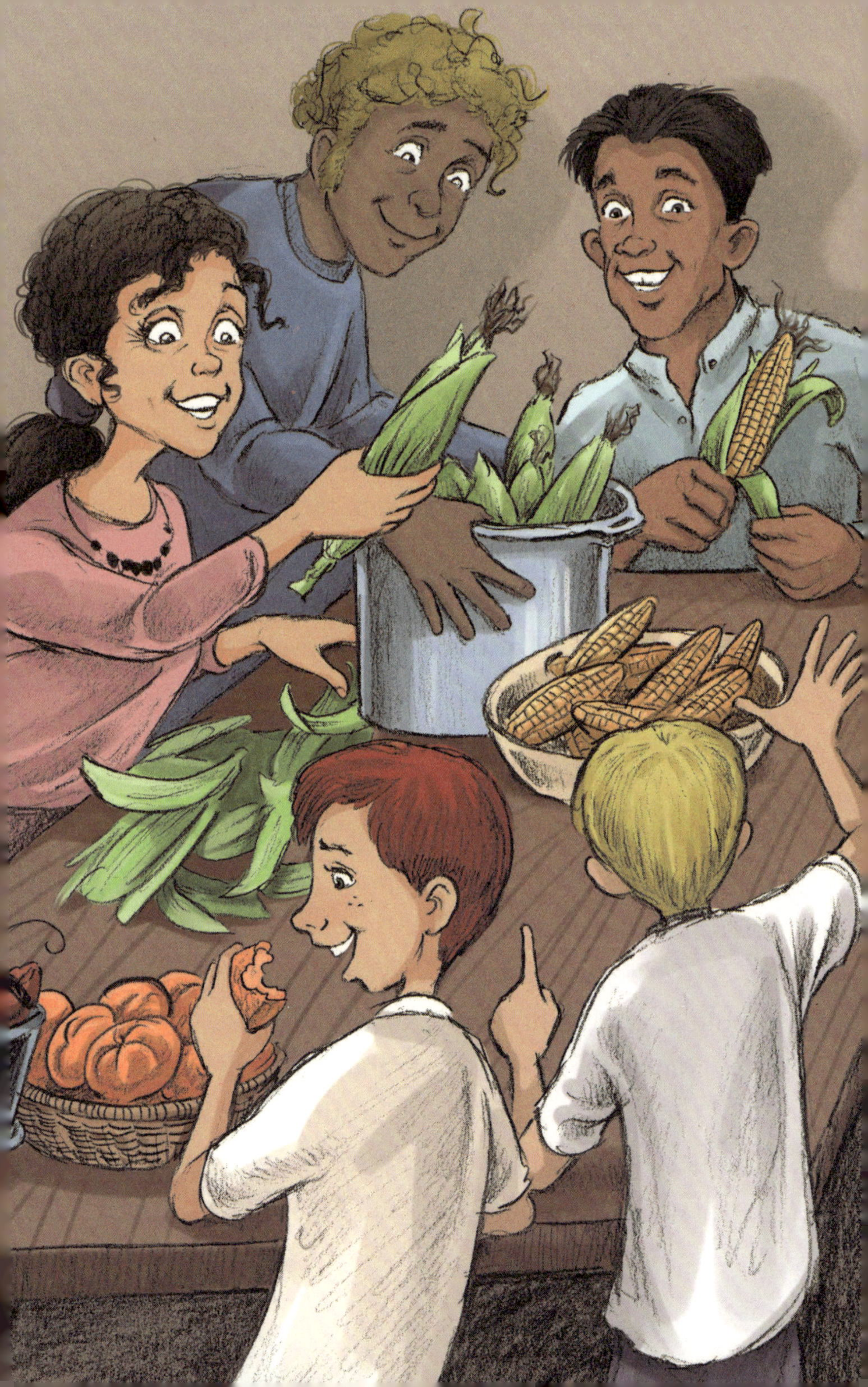

idea to himself.

"Well, I have lobsters to cook," Wallis said. "I hope everyone's hungry!"

After supper, the grownups decided to play Scrabble.

"You kids can join us," Wallis said. "Or you can choose another board game from the hall closet. Help yourself."

"Um…I think I'll go upstairs and read," Josh said. He motioned for Dink and Ruth Rose to follow him. They met upstairs in the hall between the bedrooms. "Let's search up here while they're playing Scrabble," he said.

"What exactly are we looking for?" Dink asked.

"A secret door or passageway," Josh said, rapping his knuckle lightly on a wall.

"Josh, don't you think Wallis would've told us about a secret door?" Ruth Rose said.

"Maybe she doesn't know about it," Josh said.

"I guess we should look around," Dink agreed. "Something is making those weird noises."

"Let's start on the roof," Ruth Rose said.

恐怖的地牢

They walked down the hall, and Josh pushed open the narrow door.

At the top of the stairs, they opened another door. A cool breeze blew in their faces as they stepped onto the flat roof.

"Wow! You can see everything!" said Josh. "It would be neat to fly a kite up here!"

Dink stood between two granite battlements that were taller than he was. He felt like a king looking over his land.

"There's nothing up here," Josh said.

"Okay," Dink said. "Let's look downstairs."

The kids tromped back down to the hall.

Ruth Rose walked into her room while Dink and Josh searched theirs. Dink started with the closet, but found only dust and an old tennis racket.

He used the racket to poke behind the window curtains. A few spiders darted away, but nothing else.

Suddenly Josh screamed from the bathroom. "Dink, it's got me! Help!"

Dink charged into the bathroom, holding the tennis racket like a club. He looked around wildly, but the room was empty.

"Josh? Where are you?"

The shower curtain flew open. Josh stood there, grinning. "Boo!"

Dink shook his head. "You're so lame, Josh. It would serve you right if some ghost did get you!"

Josh climbed out of the tub. "Thought you didn't believe in ghosts, Dinkus!"

Dink just shook his head again. He crossed the hall and knocked on Ruth Rose's door. "Find anything?" he asked.

She shook her head. "Nope."

She and Dink searched the long hall. They looked behind the radiators and inside plant pots and one tall umbrella stand.

Josh tapped on the walls, listening for hollow sounds. Finally they gave up, sweaty and dusty.

"I don't know where else to search," Dink said.

"We didn't check out the downstairs rooms," Josh said.

"We'll have to wait till tomorrow," Ruth Rose said, yawning. "I'm going to bed. And I hope I don't dream about ghosts, thanks to Josh Pinto!"

Josh grinned. "I read somewhere that ghosts eat girls with curls."

"Just let one try!" she said, then slammed her door.

Dink and Josh climbed into bed. A few minutes later they were both asleep.

Dink woke suddenly, his heart thumping. He looked at the clock. It was midnight!

Dink climbed out of bed and tiptoed to the window. He saw black trees against a blacker sky.

Then he saw it—a ghostly light near the playhouse!

Chapter 6

Dink gulped and felt goose bumps climbing his legs. Could it be Emory Scott's ghost?

The light winked a few more times, then disappeared.

Dink shivered, rubbing his eyes. When the light didn't return, he crawled back into bed.

He yawned and closed his eyes, deciding that he had seen a firefly.

But just before falling off to sleep, Dink opened his eyes again. He had seen only one light moving out there in the darkness.

Why would there be only one firefly in the woods? He thought about that until he fell asleep.

Dink dreamed that he was in the cave again. It was pitch dark. Up ahead, he heard a hideous scream. But this time, the scream didn't stop, it just got louder. Suddenly bats were flying in his face. But these bats had feathers—bright green feathers!

Dink bolted upright in his bed. The blankets were twisted around his legs and the alarm clock was buzzing.

I'm not in a cave, Dink realized. I'm still in the castle. Relieved, he shut off the alarm.

"Josh, wake up," he said.

Josh opened an eye. "Why?"

Dink climbed out of bed. "Walker's taking us lobstering, remember?" He turned on the light and yanked Josh's covers off.

"Come on, let's go catch a lobster!"

Josh groaned, but he climbed out of bed. "I hate lobsters."

Dink laughed. "You ate one last night." He pulled

on yesterday's jeans and a warm sweatshirt over his T-shirt. "I'm going downstairs. Don't go back to bed!"

Dink crossed the hall and tapped on Ruth Rose's door. She was up and dressed in yellow from top to bottom.

"Did you see anything strange last night?" Dink asked.

Ruth Rose was pulling a brush through her hair. She shook her head.

"Well, I did! I'll tell you about it downstairs."

There was a light on in the kitchen. Dink saw juice glasses, cereal bowls, and some muffins on the table. He was munching when Ruth Rose and Josh came in.

"Guys, I think someone was creeping around outside last night," Dink said. He told them about the light he'd seen in the woods.

Josh grabbed a muffin and bit off half.

"Told you," he said, trying to grin and chew at the same time. "It was Emory's ghost!"

"Very funny, Josh," Ruth Rose said.

Just then there was a thump in the mud room and the kitchen door crashed open. Josh nearly fell out of his chair.

Walker came in wearing tall rubber boots and a yellow slicker. "Ready to go?" he asked.

Dink laughed in relief. "Josh thought you were a ghost," he said.

"Did not," Josh muttered.

They walked outside and climbed into Walker's Jeep. The sky was pitch black. Dink peered into the woods, half expecting to see the strange light again.

A few minutes later Walker turned into his driveway. They got out and walked behind the house to the dock. Their feet made hollow noises on the wooden boards.

"Watch your step out here," Walker said, aiming a flashlight at Dink's feet.

Dink breathed in the salty night air. A few stars made pinpoints of light above the boat. Somewhere, he heard a night bird call.

"Ready to come aboard?" Walker asked.

Dink, Josh, and Ruth Rose followed Walker onto the dark boat.

Chapter 7

"Better slip one of those on," Walker said when they were aboard. He pointed at orange life jackets hanging on a row of pegs.

The kids climbed into the bulky vests and sat on benches. Walker started the motor, and the small boat moved away from the dock.

"It'll be about an hour before we get to my pots," Walker hollered over the roar of the engine. "Get comfortable!"

Ruth Rose and Josh curled up on the benches, but

恐怖的地牢

Dink sat up. He didn't want to miss a thing. He could smell the lobster bait. Waves slapped against the hull as they chugged through the black water.

Dink watched the glow of morning color the horizon pale yellow. It made him remember the light he'd seen last night. Did the light have anything to do with the strange noises or the two green feathers?

The boat's gentle rocking made Dink feel sleepy. He closed his eyes. Then Walker was shaking him. Dink sat up and squinted into sunlight.

The waves rocked the boat back and forth. When Dink stood, he nearly lost his balance. "Where are we?" he asked.

"About five miles out," Walker said. "Wake up Ruth Rose and Josh, and we'll eat."

They sat in a patch of sunlight. Breakfast was peanut butter sandwiches and hot, milky cocoa from Walker's thermos.

Dink saw other boats in the distance. "Are those all lobster boats?"

Walker nodded. "Most of them are. A few fishing boats are out, too."

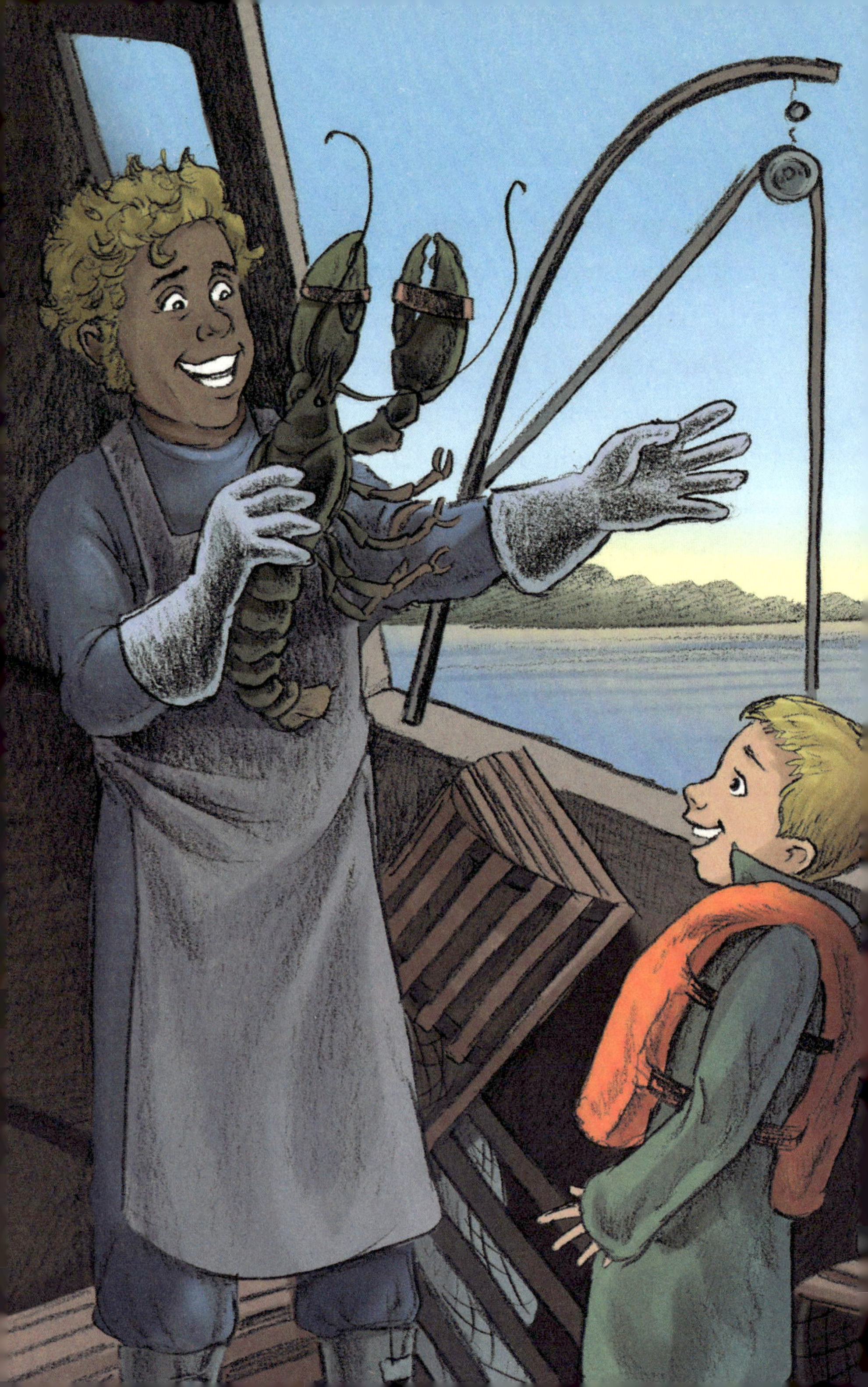

Josh looked over the side. "How do you catch the lobsters?" he asked.

Walker pointed to a machine. "That winch brings them up. I'll show you how it works."

Walker picked up a long pole with a hook on one end. He used it to grab the rope attached to a marker buoy. He snagged the rope onto the winch, pushed a button, and wet rope began whistling up out of the water. Fast!

A few seconds later a lobster pot surfaced on the other end of the rope. Wearing a rubber apron and gloves, Walker dragged it into the boat.

The wooden trap was covered with seaweed. A few small crabs scampered out onto the deck. "Let's see what we've got," Walker said, dropping the crabs back into the sea.

Walker opened the pot's small door and reached in a gloved hand. He pulled out a wet, dark green lobster. The lobster waved its claws angrily.

"Those claws can break a finger," Walker warned. He snapped two thick rubber bands onto the lobster's front claws. Then he dropped the lobster into a tank of sea water.

"Josh, get the bait, will you?"

Josh dragged the heavy pail over. Walker pulled out a huge fish head.

"Oh, phew!" Josh said. "That's gross!"

"The lobsters don't mind," Walker said, dropping

the fish head into the lobster pot. He fastened the door and shoved the trap back into the water.

"That's pretty much how it's done," Walker said, slapping water off his gloves.

"Can we pull another one?" Dink asked.

"Sure, and you guys can help. Grab some gloves out of that locker."

Ruth Rose brought out three pairs of thick rubber gloves. Walker winched up another pot and held a wiggling lobster out to Josh.

"Hold him by the back so he can't reach you with his claws."

Josh held the lobster with both gloved hands. Ruth Rose and Dink snapped rubber bands onto the claws.

"Who wants to put bait in the pot?" Walker asked, grinning.

Dink volunteered while Josh faked gagging noises. Dink stuck his hand into the bait bucket, then dropped a bloody fish head into the lobster pot.

The morning grew warm, so the kids stripped off their sweatshirts. The ocean was calm. Sea gulls soared overhead, watching for scraps.

"Look, there's Rip," Walker said.

Rip pulled his boat up next to Lady Luck. When the boats were side by side, Rip tossed a line to Dink.

"How's it going?" Rip asked. He was wearing clean jeans and a T-shirt. He held a coffee mug in one hand.

"We got a few," Walker said. "My crew here was a big help."

"Are you going lobstering?" Josh asked.

Rip shook his head and flashed a grin. "Not today, kiddo. Just came out to check my buoys. Toss me the line, okay?"

Dink tossed his end of the rope toward the other boat. Rip caught it in his free hand. "Have a good day!" he yelled as he pulled away.

"Anyone want more cocoa?" Walker asked.

"I do," Josh said.

Dink turned around and saw something on Lady Luck's deck.

It was a bright green feather.

Chapter 8

Dink snatched up the feather. Ruth Rose raised her eyebrows. Dink shrugged and stuck the feather in his pocket.

"Ready to head in?" Walker asked. "I promised Sis I'd get you back before lunch."

He started up the engine, and they chugged toward land.

Back at Walker's dock, the kids helped him hose fish goo and seaweed off the deck of his boat. Then he drove them to the castle.

"Sis's car is gone," Walker said. "She must be out doing errands. Will you kids be okay for a while?"

"I'm a little hungry," Josh said, grinning.

"Here, finish this." Walker handed Josh the bread, peanut butter, and knife. He waved and drove away.

"Where should we eat?" Josh asked.

"How about the playhouse?" Ruth Rose said. "I can wash those little dishes." She found a watering can next to the mud room door and filled it from the spigot.

On the way to the playhouse, Dink pulled the feathers out of his pocket. He told Josh how he'd found the third one on Walker's boat.

The kids studied the feathers, holding them up to the sunlight. "They're exactly alike," Josh said.

"Another parrot feather?" Ruth Rose asked. "Where could they be coming from?"

Josh grinned. "From a parrot?"

"Very funny, Joshua!"

Dink suddenly remembered his dream. Screaming bats with green feathers…

Ruth Rose opened the playhouse door and they

walked in.

"It's too cold in here," Josh said. "Why don't we eat out in the sun?"

Dink helped Josh carry the table out.

Ruth Rose brought out the dishes and set them in the grass.

"The rug looks pretty dusty," Dink said. "We should drag it outside and sweep it."

Josh was spreading peanut butter on bread at the table. "Can we eat first, then work? My stomach is talking to me."

On his knees, Dink began rolling up the rug. "Your stomach is—hey, guys, look!"

"Not another green feather, I hope," Josh muttered. He strolled over to see.

Dink pointed to a trapdoor in the floor.

"Yes!" Josh yelled. "I told you! The secret door to the secret dungeon!"

Ruth Rose ran over. "Let's open it!" she said.

The handle had a spring lock. Ruth Rose squeezed the spring, and the lock popped open. With all three of them pulling, they were able to raise the trapdoor.

They heard a creepy whoosh, then cold, damp air escaped.

"Yuck, what a smell!" Josh said.

The kids stared into the musty-smelling hole. Stone steps led down to darkness. Even in the dim light, they saw footprints on the steps.

"Just like the prints we saw on the rug," Dink said.

They all jumped back as a hollow scream echoed out of the dark hole.

Chapter 9

"Something's down there!" Ruth Rose whispered.

Josh's eyes were huge. "Not something," he whispered. "Someone. It's the ghost of Emory Scott!"

Dink put his hand in his pocket and felt the three green parrot feathers.

Taking a deep breath, he put a foot on the top step. "I'm going down," he said.

Dink walked down the steps, feeling along the cold stone walls. He tried not to think about slimy things that hung out in damp tunnels.

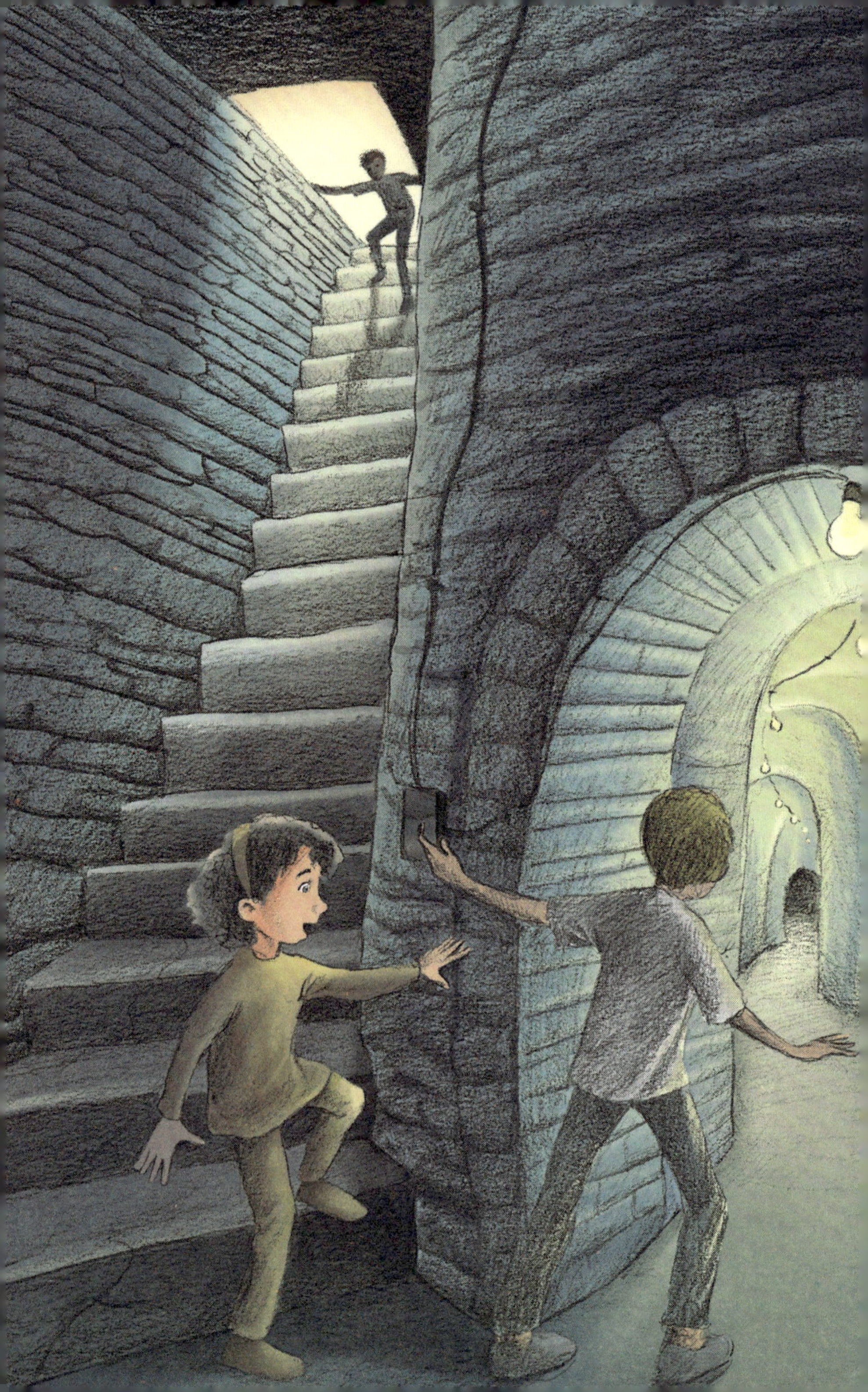

Then his hand touched something square and hard. A light switch! He flipped it up, and the space was suddenly flooded with light.

"It's a long tunnel!" he yelled.

Ruth Rose hurried down the steps. She turned to Josh. "Coming?"

"All right," Josh sighed. "But if anything touches me, I'm out of here!"

The tunnel was cold and narrow. They walked along the dirt floor. Small, cobweb-covered light bulbs hung from the ceiling. The air smelled rotten.

The tunnel went straight for a while, then turned a corner.

"Listen," Ruth Rose said. "I hear water."

"I hate this," Josh said. "I really do."

Dink turned the corner and found himself standing in water. Something let out a screech, and Dink froze.

Josh grabbed Dink around the neck. "What the heck was that?" he squeaked.

"Josh, you're strangling me!" Dink croaked.

"Sorry," Josh said.

"Where are we?" Ruth Rose asked.

A to Z 神秘案件

They were standing at the entrance to a cave. The rock walls oozed, and the floor was under water. Off to the left, another tunnel continued out of sight.

"I think I know where we are," Dink whispered.

"Me too," Josh said. "We're in the dungeon. I'd better not see any skeletons!"

"I think if we'd kept going through the cave yesterday," Dink continued, "we'd have ended up here."

"It's one long tunnel," Ruth Rose said. "From the playhouse to the ocean!"

Then something behind them made a loud squawk.

Josh jumped, nearly knocking Dink over.

"Look, guys," Ruth Rose said. "Over there!" She pointed to a dark mound up against one wall.

Dink walked over, splashing through the cold water.

"It's a tarp," he said.

Holding his breath, Dink grabbed one corner and yanked it away. Under the tarp were two cages, one on top of the other. Each cage held four large green parrots.

The birds panicked, beating their wings against

the cage bars. Their screams echoed again and again off the cave walls.

"So much for the ghost of Emory Scott," Ruth Rose said.

Josh laughed. "Good! I don't know what I'd have done if I'd bumped into him!"

Dink pulled the feathers from his pocket. He held them next to one of the parrots.

"They're the same," he said.

"What the heck is this place?" Ruth Rose asked. "Who'd hide parrots in a cave?"

"I don't know," Dink said.

"Guys!" Ruth Rose said. She was looking down. "The tide must be coming in. The water is getting deeper!"

Dink and Josh looked down. The water was up to their ankles!

"The parrots!" Josh said.

The bottom cage was getting wet. The parrots shrieked at the rising water.

"Let's get them outside!" Dink said, grabbing the top cage. He lugged it into the dry tunnel.

Josh and Ruth Rose took the other cage. They hurried back along the tunnel with the parrots squawking in fear.

Dink stopped at the bottom of the stone steps and looked up. "Uh-oh."

"What?" Ruth Rose gasped.

"I thought we left the trapdoor open," Dink said.

"We did," Josh said.

"Well, it's closed now." Dink set his cage on the floor. He walked up the steps and pushed on the door. It didn't budge.

Josh climbed the steps, and they both shoved against the door.

"It's no use," Dink said. "The door must have fallen, and the lock snapped shut."

"What can we do?" Ruth Rose asked. "If the tide floods this tunnel…"

Dink walked back down the steps. "There's another way out. But we'll have to swim."

Chapter 10

"Where?" Ruth Rose asked.

"We can go back to the cave and swim out through the tunnel," Dink explained.

"But there are bats in there!"

"It's our only way out," Josh said.

The kids lugged the two cages back through the tunnel. The parrots screeched and beat their wings.

In the cave, the water was almost up to their knees, and rising.

"We better get out of here fast," Josh said.

A to Z 神秘案件

Ruth Rose peered into the other tunnel. "I wonder how far it is to the beach," she said.

"It can't be that far," Dink said. "We're probably right under the castle."

"How are we gonna swim and carry these cages at the same time?" Josh asked. He glanced around the dark cave. "We need a raft or something."

"If the water's not too deep, we can walk out," Dink said.

He handed his cage to Ruth Rose, then stepped into the deeper water. It came up to his waist.

"It's kind of cold," he said, shivering, "but it's not very deep. We can carry the cages out."

"But what if it gets deeper?" Josh asked. "We can't carry the cages on our heads!"

"I have an idea," Ruth Rose said. "I read it in a *Girl Scout* magazine. It showed how to use your jeans as floats. You can make water wings by tying knots in the ankles and legs."

"You mean get undressed?" Josh said. "No way!"

"That's a great idea," Dink said. He climbed back out of the deep water, then kicked out of his sneakers and wet jeans. He tied knots in his jeans and put his sneakers back on.

Dink looked at Josh. "Come on," he said. "The water's getting deeper."

"Okay, but I feel weird," Josh muttered, pulling off his sneakers and jeans. The water reached just below his boxer shorts.

Dink tied knots in Josh's jeans, then dropped both pairs into the water. The air-filled jeans floated!

"Ready?" Dink said. They stepped into the water and balanced the two cages on top of the floating jeans.

"It works!" said Ruth Rose.

"This water's cold and yucky," Josh said.

"At least we can touch bottom," Dink said. "Okay, let's go."

The tunnel grew darker as they waded away from the cave. The water reached their chests, but got no higher.

The parrots were quiet, as if they knew they were being rescued.

"Do you think there are sharks in here?" Josh said.

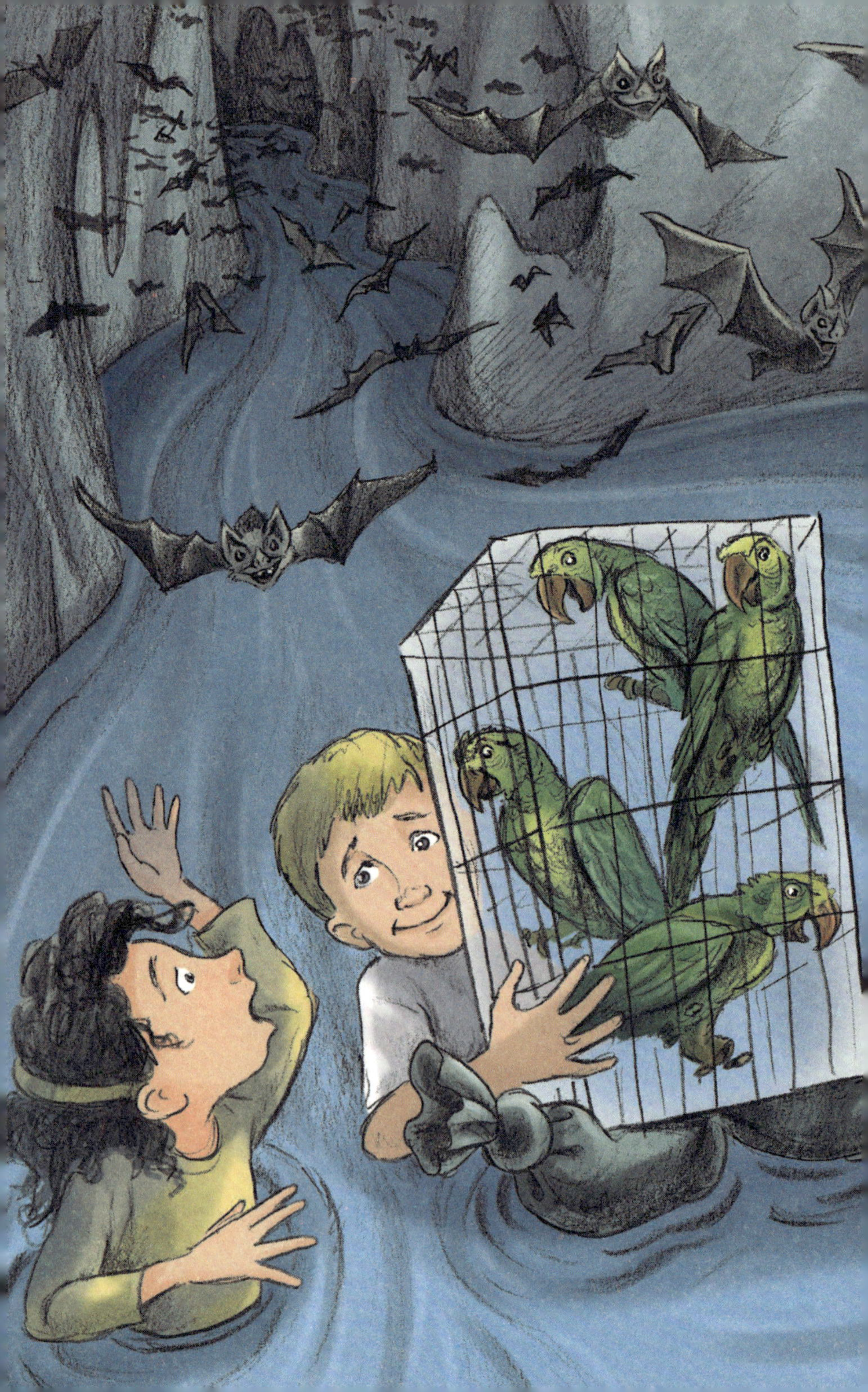

His voice echoed.

"No," Dink said. "Just a few man-eating lobsters."

Suddenly they heard a whispery sound in the darkness around them.

"What's that?" Ruth Rose asked.

"Calm down," Josh said, giggling. "It's just bats. We must've scared them."

"Are they friendly?" asked Ruth Rose.

"Not if you're an insect," Josh said.

Finally they saw daylight. Ahead was the ocean end of the tunnel.

"We did it, guys!" Dink said. They dragged the cages and soggy jeans to the beach near where they'd eaten their picnic.

"Boy, does the sun feel good!" Josh said, flopping down on the sand.

The kids rested and caught their breath. Dink and Josh took the knots out of their jeans and spread them out to dry.

"I was thinking about these parrots," Josh said. "I have a book about endangered birds, and I think these guys are in it."

"Why would anyone hide endangered parrots in a cave?" Ruth Rose asked.

"Poachers," Josh said, pulling off his soaked sneakers. "Poachers catch rare animals and sell them for a lot of money."

"But who?"

Josh shrugged. "Someone who knows about the tunnel."

恐怖的地牢

"I think I know who it is," Dink said.

Josh and Ruth Rose looked at him.

"Who?" Josh asked.

Dink looked sad. "Walker Wallace."

Chapter 11

"WHAT?" Ruth Rose yelled. "That's crazy!"

Dink shrugged. "I found one of the feathers in his Jeep and another on his boat."

Josh nodded slowly. "And when we had our picnic here yesterday, Wallis said Walker had been in the cave. Maybe he found the trapdoor in the playhouse."

"The footprints on the rug were big enough to be his," Dink said.

Ruth Rose stood up and wiped sand off her wet jeans. "I don't believe you guys. Walker wouldn't break the law! And he sure wouldn't use his sister's house!"

"I hope not," Dink said. "Anyway, let's get the parrots up to the castle."

Dink and Josh tugged on their damp jeans and grabbed the cages. A few minutes later they burst into Wallis's kitchen.

She was writing at the table.

"We found out what's making those noises!" Dink blurted out.

The kids told Wallis about the tunnel to the cave and the parrots.

"A trapdoor in the playhouse!" Wallis exclaimed with wide eyes. "And a tunnel? How incredible!"

"It's like a secret passageway," Josh said. "Maybe pirates hid gold down there!"

"Well, I don't know about pirates," Wallis said. "But now I know how Emory Scott got all that marble and stuff up here!"

"What should we do with the parrots?" asked Ruth Rose.

"Show me," Wallis said.

They all trooped into the mud room. When the door opened, the parrots began flapping around in the cages. Their shrieks filled the room.

"Poor things," Wallis said. "Should we feed them? What do parrots eat?"

"Got any fruit?" Josh said. "That's what they'd eat in the rain forests."

Wallis went to the kitchen.

"I wonder where these guys came from," said Ruth Rose.

Josh studied the parrots. "Probably Africa or South America," he said.

"How would the poachers get them all the way to Maine?" Dink asked.

"By boat," Josh said. "Then a smaller boat would bring them into the cave."

"A boat like Walk—"

Dink stopped talking as Wallis came back with two peeled bananas and a bunch of grapes. They dropped the fruit into the cages. The parrots grabbed the food in their beaks.

"They were starving!" Wallis said. She placed a

bowl of water in each cage.

"I'm kind of hungry, too," Josh said. "We missed lunch."

"Well, we can't have that!" Wallis said. "Come into the kitchen."

While she made sandwiches, Dink explained about the light he'd seen in the woods the night before. "I bet there were more cages. They must take them out through the playhouse at night."

"We should hide down there and see who it is!" Ruth Rose said.

Wallis shook her head. "Absolutely not. Those people could be dangerous!"

She brought out plates and napkins. "Today is Sunday, but tomorrow morning I'm going to call the state capitol. They must have someone who deals with poachers."

Wallis looked at the kids. "Promise me you'll stay out of that tunnel and cave."

Dink kicked Ruth Rose and Josh under the table.

"We promise," he said.

After lunch, the kids went back to the playhouse.

157

They cleaned the dishes and swept the rug.

"I wish we could get these poacher guys," Dink said.

"I think we should sleep in the playhouse," Josh said. "Then if anyone comes, we'll grab them!"

"Josh, they'd grab us and stick us in a cage," Ruth Rose said.

"Besides, Wallis would never let us stay down here," Dink said. "But I have another idea!"

At one-thirty in the morning, the kids were crouched by the window in Dink and Josh's dark room. They were fully dressed.

Josh yawned. "Maybe no one is coming tonight."

"Maybe they know we found the cages," Dink said. "Walker could've seen us from his boat."

"I still don't think it's Walker," Ruth Rose said. "But whoever it is will have to come to feed the parrots, right?"

"Right," Dink said. "Let's take turns watching. I'll go first. You guys can snooze."

"Wake me up if you see any bad guys!" Josh said,

恐怖的地牢

flopping on his bed.

"Well, I'm not tired," Ruth Rose said. "I hope they go to jail for a hundred years!"

She and Dink stared out into the darkness. The alarm clock counted away the minutes.

Josh began snoring.

"Look," Ruth Rose whispered a while later. "A firefly."

Dink saw a light moving slowly through the darkness. "Wake Josh," he told her. "That's no lightning bug!"

The kids tiptoed past Wallis's room, then hurried down the steps and out through the mud room door. Creeping silently, they approached the playhouse.

Moonlight fell on the clearing. A few yards from the playhouse, a dark car stood in the shadows.

Dink grabbed Josh and Ruth Rose and pointed. It was Walker's Jeep!

"I guess you were right," Ruth Rose whispered sadly.

The kids inched forward. Suddenly Dink saw a light coming from the playhouse.

A to Z 神秘案件

A man was bent over, pulling open the trapdoor! A glowing flashlight lay on the floor next to his feet.

The man stood up. In the flashlight's beam, Dink recognized who it was.

Ruth Rose grabbed his arm. "Ripley Pearce!" she whispered.

A moment later, Rip disappeared down the steps into the tunnel.

Suddenly Josh bolted around the corner of the

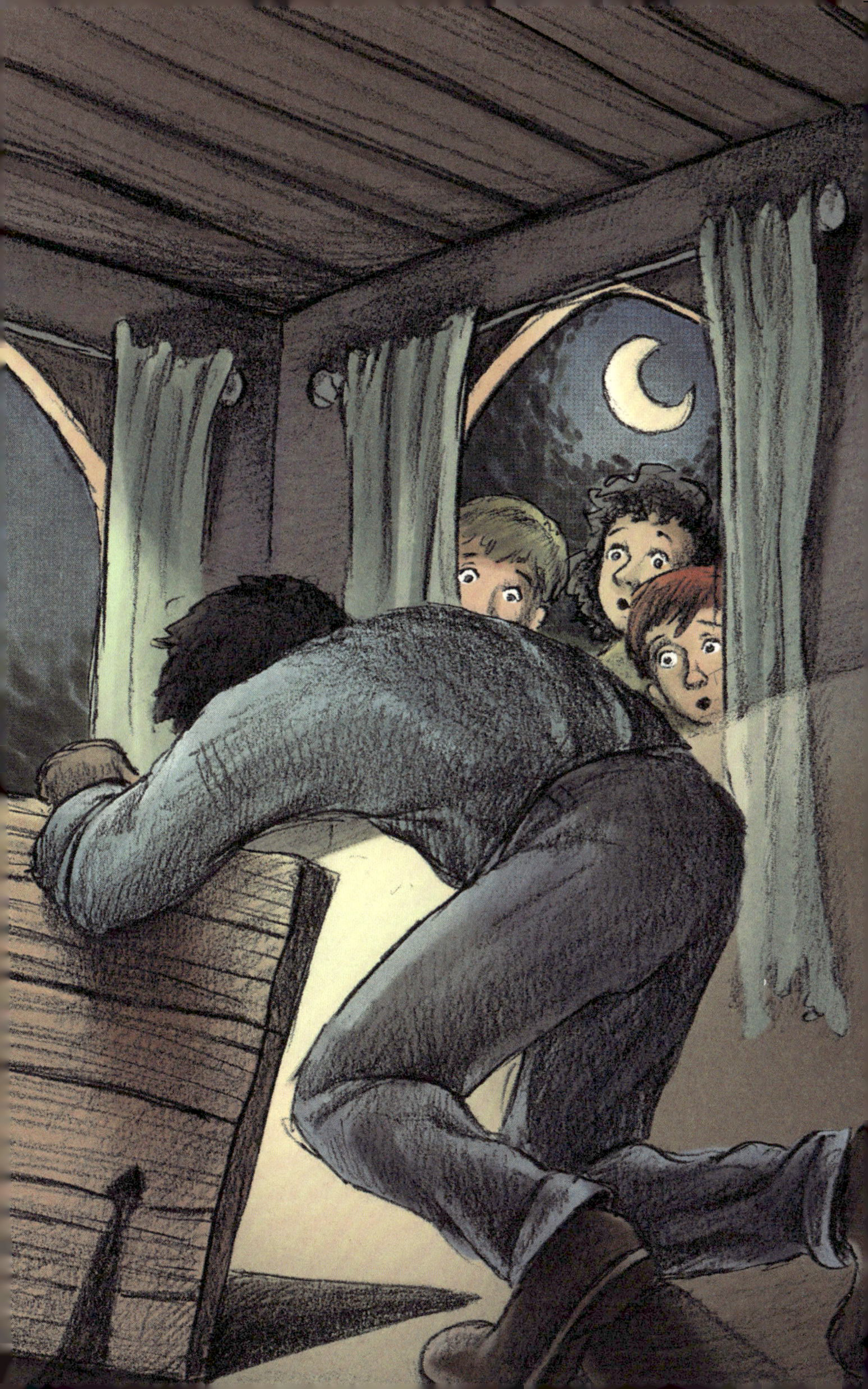

playhouse and through the open door.

   Before Dink could say anything, Josh slammed the trapdoor shut. Dink heard the spring lock snap into place.

Chapter 12

"What's Operation Game Thief?" Dink asked the next day.

"It's an 800 number you can call in Maine to report poachers," Wallis explained. She brought more hot pancakes to the table.

No one had gotten much sleep. After locking the trapdoor, Dink, Josh, and Ruth Rose had run back to wake up Wallis. She'd called 911 and reported poachers on her property.

The police had come and arrested Rip. The

officers gave Wallis the Operation Game Thief phone number.

Wallis had then driven Walker's Jeep to his house and brought him back to the castle.

"The Maine Fish and Game Department will have plenty of questions for Rip," Walker said. "Trading in endangered animals is a federal crime."

"How did Rip get the parrots?" Josh asked.

"He must have contacts in the countries where they were captured," Walker said. "The police will be checking his phone bills to see whom he called."

"He probably used his own lobster boat," Wallis said, shaking her head. "No wonder it always looked so clean."

"Why did he have your Jeep?" Josh asked.

Walker speared another pancake. "Rip's car conked out a few days ago, so I let him borrow mine."

"It was a perfect set-up," Wallis said. "Rip needed money, and he had contacts who would pay a lot for rare parrots."

"I wonder if he sold any other animals," Josh said, "like monkeys or snakes."

"We may find out yet," Walker said. He winked at Josh. "What made you decide to shut the trapdoor on Rip?"

"I got mad!" Josh said. "I wanted him to see how it felt to be in a cage."

"So that green feather on Josh's sneaker came from Rip, right?" Dink asked.

Walker nodded. "He probably brought it into the Jeep on his foot. And the one you found on my boat got there the same way."

Josh blushed. "For a while we thought you were the poacher," he told Walker.

"Well, I never did!" Ruth Rose said. Walker grinned at Ruth Rose. "Thanks! What made you so sure?"

"You're too busy," she answered. "And you wouldn't be mean to parrots. You threw those little crabs back in the water yesterday."

"What will happen to the parrots?" Dink asked.

"I assume they'll go back to where they came from," Walker said. "And Rip will most likely go to jail."

"And thanks to you kids, I won't have to hear any

more strange noises," Wallis said.

She grinned shyly. "But to tell the truth, I think I'll miss the ghost of Emory Scott. I kind of liked living in a haunted castle!"

Just then a loud screech came from the mud room.

Text copyright © 1998 by Ron Roy
Cover art copyright © 2015 by Stephen Gilpin
Interior illustrations copyright © 1998 by John Steven Gurney
All rights reserved. Published in the United States by Random House Children's Books,
a division of Random House LLC, a Penguin Random House Company, New York.
Originally published in paperback by Random House Children's Books, New York, in 1998.

本书中英双语版由中南博集天卷文化传媒有限公司与企鹅兰登（北京）文化发展有限公司合作出版。

"企鹅"及其相关标识是企鹅兰登已经注册或尚未注册的商标。
未经允许，不得擅用。
封底凡无企鹅防伪标识者均属未经授权之非法版本。

©中南博集天卷文化传媒有限公司。本书版权受法律保护。未经权利人许可，任何人不得以任何方式使用本书包括正文、插图、封面、版式等任何部分内容，违者将受到法律制裁。

著作权合同登记号：字18-2023-258

图书在版编目（CIP）数据

恐怖的地牢 ：汉英对照 / （美）罗恩·罗伊著 ；
（美）约翰·史蒂文·格尼绘 ；王芬芬译 . -- 长沙 ：湖
南少年儿童出版社，2024.10. -- （A to Z 神秘案件）.
ISBN 978-7-5562-7817-6

Ⅰ. H319.4

中国国家版本馆CIP数据核字第20241K1P64号

A TO Z SHENMI ANJIAN KONGBU DE DILAO
A to Z神秘案件 恐怖的地牢

[美] 罗恩·罗伊 著　　[美] 约翰·史蒂文·格尼 绘　　王芬芬 译

责任编辑：唐 凌　李 炜	策划出品：李 炜　张苗苗　文赛峰
策划编辑：文赛峰	特约编辑：张晓璐
营销编辑：付 佳　杨 朔　周晓茜	封面设计：霍雨佳
版权支持：王媛媛	版式设计：马睿君
插图上色：河北传图文化	内文排版：马睿君

出 版 人：刘星保
出　　版：湖南少年儿童出版社
地　　址：湖南省长沙市晚报大道89号
邮　　编：410016
电　　话：0731-82196320
常年法律顾问：湖南崇民律师事务所　柳成柱律师
经　　销：新华书店
开　　本：875 mm × 1230 mm　1/32　　印　刷：三河市中晟雅豪印务有限公司
字　　数：98千字　　　　　　　　　　印　张：5.25
版　　次：2024年10月第1版　　　　　印　次：2024年10月第1次印刷
书　　号：ISBN 978-7-5562-7817-6　　定　价：280.00元（全10册）

若有质量问题，请致电质量监督电话：010-59096394　团购电话：010-59320018